THE DEATH
OF
CHRIST

THE DEATH
OF
CHRIST

*The Cross in New Testament History
and Faith*

John Knox

Abingdon Press
NEW YORK • NASHVILLE

THE DEATH OF CHRIST

Copyright © MCMLVIII by Abingdon Press

Library of Congress Catalog Card Number: 58-5389

SET UP, PRINTED, AND BOUND BY THE
PARTHENON PRESS, AT NASHVILLE,
TENNESSEE, UNITED STATES OF AMERICA

Foreword

ALTHOUGH THIS BOOK GIVES SOME ATTENTION TO THE THREE
facets of its august theme—namely, the external circumstances
of Jesus' death, its meaning for him, and its meaning in and for
the early Church—the reader will see at once that this attention
is by no means equally divided. The short opening chapter,
concerned with the external historical conditions, does not
presume to be more than an introductory sketch; and the last
three chapters on the meaning of the Cross for the early Church
also comprise a relatively small section of the book. By far the
largest attention is given to the problem of the central chapters,
the problem of Jesus' own understanding of his death—which
is, of course, a part of the broader problem of his understanding
of himself and his mission.

The reasons for this fuller discussion of this aspect of our
theme I shall speak of in a moment. Just now I want only to say
that, from my point of view, the third section of this book,
although relatively short, is the most important. In both of the
first two sections we are dealing with questions which must
be answered on the basis of the criticism of documents—
which means that they cannot be very surely answered and
also that the answers cannot, in the nature of the case, be of
ultimate or decisive importance. It is not until we reach the

7

third section that we come to the ultimately significant element in our theme—the meaning of the death of Christ in early Christian memory, life, and thought. For, as will be said again later, by the Cross we mean neither the execution of a Roman political prisoner nor the tragic end of a uniquely noble and dedicated life, but rather the central moment in a divine event which only the Church remembers and the continuing meaning of which only the Church can know. It is only when we turn to a consideration of that meaning that the context in which earlier discussions have any great importance clearly appears. I feel, therefore, more than the author's usual interest that those who begin this book will find it possible to read on to the end.

The reasons why I have felt justified in giving largest attention to the subject of the middle section, "Jesus and His Cross," are chiefly, I suppose, its controversial nature and the fact that the problem of the "messianic consciousness" of Jesus, a perennial problem, is now again a matter of lively interest in many theological circles. But I have also a more practical purpose. I believe it is a real service to the memory of Jesus to question some of the thoughts about himself which are commonly attributed to him. Ordinarily it is true, I fear—and perhaps especially just now in the current phase of theological discussion—that one who argues, as I shall do, that Jesus probably did not make the kind of claims for himself which the Gospels make for him is thought of as in some way depreciating Jesus or detracting from his greatness. I believe that exactly the reverse is true. In making my argument, I hope I am moved principally by an interest in the truth, but I am certainly moved also by the conviction that some of the traditional conceptions of Jesus' self-consciousness reflect seriously (of course without intending to or knowing that they do) either upon his sanity or goodness as a human being or upon

8

the authenticity of his humanity itself. I think it important to show if possible that the Gospels, critically examined, do not provide a basis for disparagements or doubts on any of these scores.

Although what is presented in these pages was planned from the beginning as a single book and was written with readers, rather than hearers, especially in mind, my work on it was begun in preparation for the Shaffer Lectures, which were delivered at the Divinity School of Yale University in February of 1956. Four of the chapters are substantially identical with these lectures. The book also contains material from the Carew Lectures at the Hartford Theological Seminary in March, 1957, and from convocation lectures at the Eden Theological Seminary in the following April. I am deeply grateful for the honor conferred on me by each of these institutions, for the hospitality shown me, and for the kindness with which my words were received.

While I must, of course, take entire responsibility for this book, I want to express my warm thanks to my friend and colleague Professor Frederick C. Grant, who read the whole of my manuscript, and to other friends, Professor Paul Schubert of Yale University, Professor Wilhelm Pauck of Union Theological Seminary, and Dr. William R. Farmer of Drew University, who read sections of it. Each of these friends made valuable criticisms.

JOHN KNOX

Contents

11

I. INTRODUCTION

CHAPTER ONE

"Under Pontius Pilate"

NO ONE COULD BE SO BOLD AS TO TAKE UP THE THEME OF THIS book without misgiving. The death of Christ is the central moment in the whole event to which Christian faith and devotion look back. From the beginning it has seemed supremely to represent all the values and meanings realized within the Christian community, providing universal Christianity with its most characteristic symbol. And it has always been remembered as a moment of strange and awful pregnancy, significant beyond our understanding, pointing us toward heights incalculably beyond our reach and making us aware of depths in our existence which we know we shall never sound or probe. No wonder the sun was hidden "from the sixth hour . . . until the ninth." It is significant that, according to the Gospels, both the death of Christ and the Resurrection took place in darkness—events too sacred to be gazed on, too full of portent to be plainly seen.

And yet the recognition of this ineffable character has not kept the Church from making the Cross the center of theological interest and attention throughout its whole history, and it must not be deemed rash or presumptuous for one to seek what light one can find and to understand as fully as one can. There can be no genuine awareness of mystery except as a by-product of the search for understanding. At the end point of our questioning stands One who does not answer our questions but receives and absorbs them in the vaster mystery of his own being. But this happens only at the end point of our questioning. Only he who resolves all the mysteries he can is in position to recognize the one ultimate and all pervasive mystery which cannot be resolved. Only he who has sought earnestly to master can know when he is really mastered. Only one who has challenged all the gods can know the one true God. It is only at the very end of the New Testament's longest, most sustained, and most serious effort to understand and formulate the meaning of life and history that we read: "O the depth of the riches and wisdom and knowledge of God! How unsearchable are his judgments and how inscrutable his ways!" It is only after we have tried with the utmost seriousness and with every energy of our minds to understand that we have the right to make such a confession; it is only then that we are really able to make it. . . . So much by way of apologia for my proposal of a general theme so momentous and so sacred.

I

The particular question with which we begin, however, is furthest removed from the center of greatest significance in our theme; and our apologia, perhaps unnecessary in any case, will seem not to apply. We begin by asking what we can know about the external circumstances and the historical causes of Jesus' death. But though this is a straightforward historical query, involving remotely if at all the question of theological meaning, it is in its own way as difficult to answer as the other— not because the issues are so deep but because the evidence is so meager and, even where it exists, so ambiguous. There can be no doubt whatever, of course, that Jesus was put to death by crucifixion—on this all our sources, including Paul, agree—and this datum may almost be said to belong essentially to the Church's memory of Jesus himself. One can be almost equally sure that the Crucifixion took place in or near Jerusalem, in a Passover time, during the procuratorship of Pilate and by the hand of the Romans. But one cannot go beyond these formal facts with anything like the same assurance. Granted that the final responsibility for Jesus' death must rest with the Roman authorities, what part if any did the Jewish leaders have in bringing it about? How was Jesus tried? How many hearings were held and before whom? What were the charges against him? Of precisely what crime was he convicted? Such questions are still not answerable with complete assurance and perhaps will never be. Although the Passion narratives of the four Gospels are relatively full, they are not always consistent with one another; and even where they agree, what we know about the nature and purpose of the Gospels and about the growth of the tradition which they embody requires that we be critical. There are, moreover, significant silences. In a word, the Gospels do not provide us with a clear, consistent picture of the external historical facts of Jesus' crucifixion.

Fortunately, the purpose of this book does not require that we obtain such a picture. We are concerned primarily, not with the external circumstances of Jesus' death, but rather with the meaning the death had for Jesus himself and for the early Church. Therefore, I shall make no attempt to deal with the subject of this chapter in any thoroughgoing way. I shall not try to compare systematically the several Passion narratives or to discuss the problem of their sources or of interdependence among them. I shall not attempt to describe in detail the political situation in Palestine in the early first century or to place the career of Jesus realistically within that

17

setting. Nor shall I undertake at the end any exact reconstruction of what happened. Indeed, I shall do little more than call to mind three general tendencies operative in the Gospel tradition as a whole which must be supposed to have exercised an effect upon the way the original facts of Jesus' crucifixion were remembered and reported, and shall raise, but not try to settle, the question of the extent to which each should be taken into account in our estimation of the Gospel evidence. I have in mind, first, the tendency to draw out, to elaborate, to make "important," the incident of Jesus' crucifixion; second, the tendency to play down the Roman part in it and to emphasize correspondingly the part taken by Jews; and third, the tendency to discount the political significance of the incident. There can be no doubt that such tendencies operated; the only question is how extensive were their effects.

First, then, we must recognize the existence in the Gospel tradition of a tendency to elaborate, to "play up," the bare facts of Jesus' crucifixion. Let us imagine, quite hypothetically, that nothing was really known to have happened except that officers of a Roman military force, responsible for helping to maintain peace in Jerusalem at the time of the Passover feast in A.D. 29 or 30, observing that Jesus was the object of considerable public interest and hearing talk about the "kingdom of God," quietly arrested him one night while he was outside the city with a few friends and, after a brief hearing before the procurator, put him to death as a possible troublemaker along with others of the same kind. Can we not be sure that even if the incident as first known had been thus simple and straightforward, it would not have remained so in the Church's tradition? The crucifixion of Jesus was almost at once to become the focus of attention in both faith and worship, the center of meaning in the whole Christian gospel. It would have been

18

inconceivable that an event of such supreme significance should have happened quickly, casually, inconspicuously. Luke reports a disciple's question to a supposed stranger: "Are you the only visitor to Jerusalem who does not know the things that have happened there in these days?" (24:18). It had to be so. As the same writer says later (Acts 26:26), events so important could not have occurred "in a corner."

One must take into account also the exigencies of the Christian preaching. Paul tells us that in his preaching to the Galatians, Jesus Christ was "publicly portrayed" as crucified before their very eyes (Gal. 3:1). The Crucifixion had to be *pictured*. Men must see and feel it, imaginatively entering into the sufferings of Christ and sensing the awful significance of what happened on Calvary. The story of the Passion must be told in such fashion that the stark reality of it be felt and the full redemptive meaning of it be realized. The early preachers would have dealt with the Crucifixion, or for that matter with any other incident in the life of Jesus, not in the manner of historians, but in the manner of dramatists. We can be sure of this, if for no other reason, because preachers still deal so with the Gospel materials; and if the four Gospels had not crystallized the tradition around the end of the first century, who would venture to guess how long and elaborate the story of Jesus' crucifixion would now be? In a word, if suitable and adequate materials for the preaching were not available in the Gospel-making period, they were created. If a modern preacher finds such a statement shocking, let him watch what he himself does the next time he takes a Gospel incident for his text. Almost inevitably he will fill out the Gospel story with details and concrete touches designed to make it more graphic or moving and to bring out what he feels to be the real meaning or intention of the story. Such dramatic handling of a text is in principle legitimate as well as inevitable. And we have every reason to suppose that some of the elements in the story of Jesus' crucifixion as we have it in the Gospels are to be explained in this way.

In this same connection we must allow for some influence from the Old Testament texts which were found to be fulfilled in various details of the Passion drama. It would be a mistake to suppose that the texts were always suggested by the incidents and circumstances, and that the incidents and circumstances were never suggested by the texts. Did the division of Jesus' garments among the soldiers at the cross remind someone of Ps. 22:18: "They parted my garments among them and for my clothes they cast lots"? Or is that passage responsible for the creation of the story, or at any rate for some of the details of it? Did the fact that Jesus' legs were not broken remind someone of Ps. 34:20: "He guards all his bones so that not one of them is broken"? Or is the verse from the psalm the real source for the fact? When we remember that the only scripture for the Christians of the Gospel-making period was what we call the Old Testament and that it would have been incredible to them that an event so significant as the crucifixion of Jesus should not have been described in it, we are bound to allow for *some* influence of the Old Testament texts upon the tradition, although opinions among us will vary sharply as to how large the allowance should be.

Not only is it true that we would expect the original story of Jesus' trial and execution to become more elaborate with the telling, but it may also be said that what we know about the revolutionary political situation in Palestine in the mid–first century and about Roman methods of government, especially in such situations, does not prepare us for some of the features of the Gospel accounts. Especially surprising is the

seriousness and persistence with which Pilate seeks to escape
the necessity of giving a final judgment—the repeated delays,
the referring of the case to Herod, the attempt to make the
Jews take the responsibility, the offering of a choice between
Jesus and Barabbas, Pilate's washing of his hands, and the
like. If this hesitation is to be explained by Pilate's con-
scientious fear of condemning an innocent man and his sensitive
devotion to justice, then we must say that nothing we are
given to know otherwise about his character would prepare
us to expect it. Josephus represents him consistently as being
more than ordinarily callous and ruthless, and Philo speaks of
"his corruptions, his acts of insolence, his rapine, his habit of
insulting people, his cruelty, his continual murders of people
untried and uncondemned, and his never ending, gratuitous
and most grievous inhumanity" (*Legatio ad Gaium* 38; see
also Luke 13:1). Hardly the sort to be worried over a possible
injustice to an accused Galilean rebel!

But if we take the position that his behavior was motivated
by concern about the political consequences of his action, his
vacillations are just as hard to understand. Let us suppose
that the Jewish leaders and populace were demanding Jesus'
death as an enemy of Caesar (as the Gospel writers tend to
see the matter); then, loyalty to the emperor and interest in
preserving the peace would seem plainly to have agreed in
dictating Jesus' execution. On the other hand, if we suppose
(as the Gospel evidence on the whole suggests) that Jesus had
a considerable popular following in Jerusalem, we must recognize that he would have seemed on this account all the more
dangerous. The presence of numerous followers might naturally have led to the arrest's being made as inconspicuously as
possible (hence perhaps the seizure outside the city and at
night and the need of a "betrayer"), but it would not have

made the necessity of firm and prompt action less imperative. Indeed, exactly the contrary would have been true.

In a word, we may well doubt the accuracy of the Gospels' accounts of Pilate's hesitations and evasions. At the very least, we must recognize the likelihood of some exaggeration. Consider the agonizing vacillations of such a man as Pilate alongside of the rather easy dispatch with which the intelligent and humane Pliny ordered the execution of some of the Christians when later in a similarly unruly province he was given reason to believe they threatened the peace! [1] Anatole France, in his story "The Procurator of Judaea," reports a conversation of the aged Pilate, now in retirement, and an old crony of his who had known him in Judea. Pilate, after discoursing for twenty pages or so about various persons and happenings belonging to the period of his procuratorship, refers to Jesus only in the final sentence of the story: "Jesus? Jesus of Nazareth? I cannot call him to mind." There is truth here, as well as irony!

How the line should be drawn in the Passion narratives between the originally remembered historical facts and the contributions of primitive imagination and faith, we shall never be able to determine with any precision or certainty. The line will be drawn further to the "right" or to the "left" by scholars equally competent. But that both elements—that is, both "history" and "interpretation"—belong to the Gospel picture, all will agree.

[1] *Letters* x. 96. It is true that Pliny had some misgivings; still he was able to write: "I have followed this method in dealing with persons accused before me as Christians. I have asked them if they were Christians. If they confessed to being such, I asked them a second and again a third time, threatening the death penalty. If they persisted, I ordered them to be executed. For I had no doubt that, whatever they had done, contumacy and inflexible obstinacy ought to be punished."

II

Some help in discriminating between the two elements will
be provided by the recognition of the second tendency mentioned at the beginning of this discussion—namely, the tendency to play down the Roman part in the execution of Jesus
and to emphasize the part taken in it by Jews. Here again there
can be no doubt of the existence of the tendency; the only
question has to do with the extensiveness of its effects. The
Gospel tradition, although it began in Palestine and bears
unmistakable marks of its origin there, soon moved into a
non-Jewish environment. Even from the beginning the most
successful evangelistic work seems to have occurred, not among
Jews, but among Gentiles; and by the time of the fall of
Jerusalem at the end of the Jewish War of A.D. 66-70, Christianity had become almost exclusively a Gentile movement.[2]
This being true, it is not surprising that, at a time when Jews
were especially under suspicion, the early Christian preachers
found the Jewish connection of their faith somewhat embar-
rassing. Their attitude, however, on this point was not simple
or unambiguous: on the one hand they prized the ancientness
of their faith, regarding it as the fulfillment of God's covenant
with Abraham and Moses—Christianity was the authentic

---

[2] Some would hold that Jewish Christianity was also steadily increasing,
perhaps at a rate equal to, or even surpassing, that maintained in the Gentile
mission, until the Jewish War put an end to both its growth and, virtually, its
existence. C. G. F. Brandon (*The Fall of Jerusalem and the Christian Church*
[London: S.P.C.K, 1951], pp. 126-53, and so on) even argues that after Paul's
arrest the Jewish church grew rapidly in importance and influence at the
expense of the Gentile church and, except for the war, might have driven
Pauline Christianity from the field. Rom. 9-11, however, seems to presuppose
that the Christian movement is largely Gentile; and Brandon, suggestive as his
book is at many points, does not convince me that it did not continue so. But
whatever be concluded as to the situation before A.D. 70, there can be no doubt
that after that date Christianity was predominantly a Gentile movement and
that the evangelists would have found its Jewish origins something of a problem.

Judaism, the true Israel—but on the other, they sought, as far as possible, to disassociate Christianity from the contemporary Jewish community. As they saw the matter, the current generation of Jews, who had rebelled against the Roman state, had earlier rebelled against their own God in rejecting the Christ whom he had sent. Indeed, the bloody defeat they had suffered at the hands of Rome was not alone a Roman punishment of their revolt, but also a divine judgment upon their disobedience and apostasy. They had "killed the Prince of life." (Acts 3:15 K.J.V.). He had come "unto his own, and his own [had] received him not" (John 1:11 K.J.V.).

And yet the unassailable fact was that Jesus had been crucified by the Romans, not stoned by the Jews. Pilate, a responsible Roman official, had ordered his execution. Under these circumstances it was inevitable that the Church should feel a strong inclination to emphasize both the reluctance of Pilate to condemn and the initiative and persistence of the Jews in urging him to do so. The arm, to be sure, was Pilate's; but the will was that of the Jewish people acting through their authorized leaders. They had demanded Jesus' death even when Pilate "had decided to release him," virtually forcing the issue upon the procurator by asking for the release of Barabbas, a "murderer" (Acts 3:13-14).

No one can study the Gospel narratives of the Passion without recognizing this tendency to exonerate the Romans and blame the Jews. But how much of the tradition is to be so explained? Are we to go so far as to say that Jews had nothing at all to do with Jesus' death—that the stories of the hearings before the high priest and the Sanhedrin and before Herod, as well as the hesitations and attempted evasions of Pilate, are simply and only products of early Christian apologetic? Some critics

24

would go as far as this. But the truth almost certainly lies somewhat short of this extreme.

The picture would be clearer if we could know whether the Sanhedrin at the time of Jesus' crucifixion held the power of death, the *ius gladii*. The Fourth Gospel definitely says that it did not (18:31) : "Pilate said to them, 'Take him yourselves and judge him by your own law.' The Jews said to him, 'It is not lawful for us to put any man to death.'" If such was really the legal situation, the whole story of Jesus' trial before the Jewish court (Mark 14:55-65 and parallels) can claim a certain degree of plausibility, for in that case we can understand how it happened that the Sanhedrin, after having tried Jesus and found him guilty of a capital crime, did not itself order and carry out his execution. On the other hand, if the Jewish authorities actually held the *ius gladii* at the time, the account of Jesus' trial before them can hardly be regarded as historical. It is not likely that they would have turned over to Pilate a case about which they were so deeply concerned if they were legally competent to handle it. Either, then, they were *not* competent or the hearing did not take place before them—unless some allowance should be made for the possibility that they had the right to deal with Jesus' case but, because of Jesus' popularity, preferred that the Romans take the responsibility of doing so. Unfortunately, the question of fact here cannot be surely answered. Eventually the *ius gladii* was certainly taken away from the Jews; it is by no means certain that this had happened as early as the time of Jesus.[3]

[3] H. Lietzmann in an influential article, "Der Prozess Jesu," *Sitzungsberichte der Preuss. Akad. der Wiss.*, Phil.-Hist. Klasse 1931 (XIV), pp. 313-22, argued persuasively that the Sanhedrin had the right of capital punishment at the time of Jesus' trial and drew the appropriate conclusions. J. Jeremias has attacked this position in "Zur Geschichtlichkeit des Verhörs Jesu vor dem Hohen Rat," *Zeitschrift für die neutestamentliche Wissenschaft* XLIII (1951), 145-50. I am inclined to think that the question has to be regarded as an open one.

We must then do without the help which reliable information on this point would give us. Perhaps the best we can do is to say that the truth probably lies somewhere between the two extremes of complete Jewish noninvolvement and the kind of complicity which the Gospels describe. The Jewish leaders, especially the priestly hierarchy, must in all probability bear some part of the responsibility for Jesus' death—after all they were as much interested in keeping the peace as Pilate was, and for the same reason (see John 11:47-50) —but certainly that part was less conspicuous and decisive than the Gospels suggest.

III

This tendency to accentuate the responsibility of the Jews is obviously closely related with the third tendency—and, for our present purpose, the most important—the tendency to discount the political significance of Jesus' crucifixion. We have already recalled that the period of Christianity's first effort to win the Gentile world coincided with the great Jewish

---

So far as John 18:31 is concerned, if it should be concluded that the Sanhedrin did have the *ius gladii*, the statement of the Fourth Evangelist to the contrary would have to be looked upon as its (no doubt sincere) attempt to explain how it could be that the highest Jewish court was so hostile to Jesus and so determined to destroy him when in actual fact he was executed by the Romans. It may be noted that John 19:6b would seem to conflict with 18:31.

The uncertainty whether the Sanhedrin had the right of death has a bearing also upon the moot question of the date of the Crucifixion. If it is supposed that the Jews had little, if anything, to do with Jesus' condemnation, there ceases to be any serious objection to the Synoptic Gospel dating of the trial and execution on the very day of the Passover. It may possibly be significant that it is the evangelist who emphasizes most strongly the role of the Jewish authorities (that is, John) who also dates the Crucifixion before the Passover. But note that J. Jeremias, who has no doubt of the important complicity of the Jewish authorities and of the trial before the Sanhedrin, still finds it possible to accept the Synoptic Gospel dating (*The Eucharistic Words of Jesus*, tr. Arnold Ehrhardt [New York: The Macmillan Co., 1955], pp. 49-53).

rebellion against the Roman state. The war itself took place in a four-year span, A.D. 66-70; but it dominates a century and more of Jewish life, not only in Palestine but throughout the world. William R. Farmer [4] has made us see that the spirit of the Maccabees, not only did not die with the coming of Roman power, but burned ever more fiercely as the years passed—that the Zealots, far from being a mere fringe group at the middle of the first century, were voicing the central hopes of Israel. A yearning for the restoration of God's sovereignty over his people—and this implied freedom from every alien yoke—was the deepest yearning in the hearts of the great masses of Jews (indeed, of all except a few Sadducean collaborationists). This does not mean that many favored immediate armed rebellion against Rome; in this respect Zealotism was a minority position. But with the basic aims of the Zealots there was general sympathy. Their characteristic cry, "No king but God," awakened a deep response in all truly Jewish hearts. The final rebellion, although it may have been precipitated by a few, was a national act—an eruption of the pent-up passions and hopes of generations of Jews.

It was in the last of these generations—a generation seething with unrest and preparing, whether it knew it or not, for the tragic denouement—that Jesus appeared as a public teacher or prophet. The burden of his message was the imminent coming of "the kingdom of God"—almost an echo of the Zealot cry. Is it strange that the Romans seized and executed him as a leader, or possible leader, of revolt? Oscar Cullmann [5] has pointed to the evidences in the Gospels that many Jews thought of him in the same way and that there were Zealots even in the

[4] *Maccabees, Zealots, and Josephus* (New York: Columbia University Press, 1956).

[5] *The State in the New Testament* (New York: Charles Scribner's Sons, 1956), pp. 8-23.

company of his disciples. To be sure, both the Romans and any Zealots in his following were mistaken in thinking that Jesus was proposing an armed revolt, and in view of the nature of Jesus' ethical teaching it is hard to see how they (particularly any of his own disciples) could have understood him so. The Kingdom was to be God's, and God would bring it to pass without any human help. But they were not mistaken in seeing—and we must not make the mistake of ignoring—the political implications of Jesus' message. The coming of the kingdom of God would mark the end of all earthly tyrannies, Rome's included and indeed above all. Whether or not this bearing of the expectation of the Kingdom was important to Jesus himself or was prominent, or even explicit, in his teaching, we cannot know; but we can be sure his hearers would not have missed it, and that it accounts for at least a part of whatever popular following he had as well as for his condemnation and execution at Roman hands.

But if we cannot avoid seeing this political significance in Jesus' crucifixion, it is equally obvious that the first Christian evangelists to the Gentiles would have had every reason for ignoring or even denying it. This would have been especially true after the war of 66-70 had emblazoned Jewish treachery and recalcitrance to all the world. The movement to interpret Jesus' message as concerned entirely with a heavenly, an otherworldly, kingdom would have begun with the beginning of the Gentile mission and would have gathered momentum as time passed. The basic facts were too well remembered and parts at least of the Passion narrative took form too early for this movement fully to succeed. The Gospel tradition does not permit us to miss the political bearings of Jesus' career. But they are certainly obscured and discounted—and, again, to an indeterminate degree. We cannot know just how far

Jesus' ideas and his career as a whole were determined by the political circumstances of his times, but we can be sure that the extent of this influence is greater than the Gospels imply.

IV

I said that I could promise no reconstruction of the circumstances of Jesus' crucifixion. And I know quite well that no clear picture emerges from what I have said. My own conviction is that no clear picture can be drawn. We can set a kind of frame of historical possibilities within which the action of the first Good Friday occurred. This we have been trying to do in this chapter. But within this frame we cannot set the action with any precision or assurance. It probably belongs somewhere in the center, midway of the several extremes; but even of this we cannot be sure.

Still, certain facts emerge clearly enough, and they are the really important ones. Jesus was announcing the imminence of the kingdom of God, a new and heavenly order which would replace all the kingdoms of this world. This was essentially a revolutionary message and was recognized as such both by the multitudes who hated the *status quo* and by the Roman authorities and their Jewish collaborators who were concerned to maintain it. Jesus was not a rebel against the state; indeed, he forbade the use of the sword and resort to any kind of coercive action. He commanded love toward the Roman enemy, as toward all others. The Kingdom would come to pass on God's initiative and in God's own time. But complete understanding of him or his intentions could hardly be expected in so disturbed a time, and officials interested only in maintaining order are never likely to pay much attention to distinctions of motive among those who seem to threaten the peace of the state. Jesus was seen as posing such a threat and on that ground was put to death. Of all this we can be virtually sure. But as to the extent Jesus' following may have included actual Zealots, as to how seriously the case was investigated by the Romans, as to what part the Jewish leaders (Pharisees as well as Sadducees) had in prosecuting it, as to how many hearings were held and just what happened in them—to all such questions our sources give no clear or certain answer.

Fortunately, as was said at the beginning, so far as the purpose of this book is concerned, this uncertainty does not greatly matter. Our concern is to understand as well as we can the inner meaning of the death, first to Jesus himself and then to the Church; and for this understanding a knowledge of the external circumstances is not decisive and often not even relevant. These circumstances are, as we have seen, furthest removed from the center of greatest significance in our theme; and we can afford—as indeed we are forced—to leave many of them in the shadow.

II. JESUS
AND HIS CROSS

CHAPTER TWO

Problem and Approach

WE ARE NOT LEAVING THE FIELD OF HISTORY IN THE NARROW or obvious sense of that word when we come to the first of the major themes we have proposed to discuss. In the previous chapter we were considering the Crucifixion in the context of what was happening in Palestine in the first century—its character as a public event. We are now to consider, at greater length and with greater care, how Jesus himself looked upon his death. What place did it have in his conception of the purpose of his life? Did it have the kind of theological meaning for him which the Church has found in it? It will be obvious at once that this question is even harder to answer than the other. Not only is the evidence again both meager and ambiguous, but also one has greater difficulty in judging it objectively since the question seems to bring us nearer to what I have called "the center of greatest significance," where the faith of the Church is actively involved. For many Christians the meaning of the Cross is by definition simply and only the meaning Jesus thought of it as having, and to raise critically the question of historical fact at this particular point is to place faith itself in jeopardy. We may recognize with the top of our mind that such an attitude is mistaken and that opening up the issue of the self-consciousness of Jesus does not involve so dire a risk, but it is hard to free ourselves entirely from the feeling that even to ask so bold a question is to enter a forbidden holy place, while to give any but the traditional answer is almost an act of desecration. Under these circumstances, those who suggest that Jesus did not share the views about himself and his death which the Gospels attribute to him, if they are not denied a hearing in advance, are often required to shoulder an impossible burden of proof.

But the problem of carrying on a reasonably objective and therefore a fruitful discussion of our theme is still further complicated by the fact that those who make this negative suggestion are likely to have a presupposition of their own. If the more conservative begin by assuming—or half assuming —that Jesus must have found the same meaning in his death that the Church has found there, the more liberal (if this is the word) are likely to start with the assumption that Jesus was not only a typical man but also in effect a modern man and that he could not have had thoughts about his death which such a man could not easily or naturally entertain. We shall not hope to be entirely free from one or the other of these presuppositions, but we shall hope to be the freer for acknowledging the falseness of both and the more ready to recognize whatever truth the evidence presents.

I

The theme of these four chapters has been a subject of controversy for a long time and involves many questions. It is obvious that we must limit our attention, and it is obviously desirable that we should focus it, as far as possible, on the crucial point in the current phase of the ongoing discussion. It is almost equally obvious what this point is. This is the claim, made by many, that Jesus wrought out a synthesis of two ideas—or found them already united—the ideas of the apocalyptic Son of man and of the Suffering Servant, and thought of himself as exemplifying and fulfilling the emergent double conception.[1] Here *is* the crucial point. If such a conception lay in Jesus' mind—if he identified the Son of man of Daniel-Enoch with the Suffering Servant of Isa. 53 and identified both with himself—then we have in Jesus' own thought, not only the primary source, but also the essential form, of later Christian thinking about the death of Christ. If the synthesis of the two conceptions as applying to Jesus was first wrought out in the experience and reflection of the early Church, then there ceases to be any reason for supposing that Jesus found any definable or recognizably Christian theological significance in his death. In stating this last conclusion so baldly, one runs the risk of being misunderstood. I do not for a moment mean that Jesus' death, in so far as he was able to anticipate it, would not have been for him, in any case, an event of profoundest spiritual meaning. It would have been the final act of obedience to the will of God to which his whole life had been so completely and singularly devoted. He would also have believed that God would use his death in some way beyond his understanding in working out his purposes. Meaning of this kind is taken for granted and will be more fully acknowledged later. The issue just now is whether Jesus con-

---

[1] The question whether, on the assumption that Jesus applied this double conception to himself, he is responsible also for the conception itself can be left open. Most scholars who take this general position feel that it was Jesus who first brought the two images together. Later in this book (see below, pp. 102-4) we must give some attention to those who argue that the synthesis had already occurred before Jesus' time. The really crucial point, however, is not whether Jesus originated the abstract conception, but whether he identified himself as the fulfillment of it; and we can leave the other question unanswered, whether now or later.

ceived of his death as an essential, predestined, and supremely significant element in the eschatological redemption, as being uniquely necessary to the salvation of either the nation or mankind, as being, in fact, the death of the Messiah of God. And with respect to this issue, the question whether he found fulfilled in himself the two images we are discussing is the decisive question.

Now the answer we give to this question undoubtedly depends to some extent upon our ways of weighing particular pieces of evidence. I am convinced, however, that it depends more largely upon the point of view from which we look at the evidence as a whole. I have in mind here not differences in theological presuppositions, although these may often lie in the background, but differences in judgment as to where the burden of proof lies when the question of historical fact is asked about sayings attributed to Jesus in the Gospels. Does it lie with those who doubt or with those who affirm? Is it "up" to those who say that the so-called historical Jesus really made this or that disputed statement to show why they think so, or is it rather the responsibility of those who deny the authenticity (in this sense) of the saying to show cause? It is obvious that one's way of answering this question may well be affected by the kind of theological presuppositions to which I have briefly referred, but any number of other factors may dispose one to the one answer or the other. I am persuaded that this difference in disposition, however caused, is of the greatest importance in discussions of such themes as we have before us, and that this difference has not been recognized and dealt with as it deserves to be. I propose to devote the present chapter to an examination of the meaning and importance of this difference, leaving to the next three whatever consideration we can give to the basic issue itself.

It is frequently said that such a question as that of, say, the miracles in the Gospels, or the so-called messianic consciousness of Jesus, or indeed any historical question having supposed theological implications—that such a question should be answered, not on the basis of our own theological presuppositions, but on the basis of the pertinent documentary evidence. On this most of us have no difficulty in agreeing. And yet when we go on to look at the evidence, we find ourselves often arriving at quite different conclusions. And this is true, probably in most cases, not because we have different evidence or even interpret it differently, but because of a difference in basic conception of where the burden of proof lies and therefore of just what or how much is to be required of the evidence.

Some of us, seeking an answer to such a question as to how Jesus thought about his death, read the Gospels in some such mood as this: "These Gospels are very primitive accounts of the life and teachings of Jesus—not biographies, perhaps, in the modern or scientific sense, but the only sources of biographical information we have. They were written within two, or at most three, generations of the time of the events they record. We have no right to distrust any of their statements unless there is good cause indeed. To be sure, these books were written for the use of the early churches and, to a degree, undoubtedly reflect their needs and interests; but this fact is to be resorted to as the explanation of a Gospel statement only where the possibility of its accuracy is clearly ruled out, and this happens very seldom. The Gospels tell us plainly that Jesus thought of his approaching suffering and death as an indispensable part of his work as Messiah and Savior. There is no reason to doubt the essential accuracy of this picture.

The burden of proof lies with those who reject it. They must show that it was impossible that Jesus should have held such a view of his death, and this they cannot do."

But others, relying just as firmly and fully upon the Gospels as sources, would express themselves somewhat differently. "The Gospels," they would say, "represent the life and faith of the churches in the final decades of the first century. It is true that they embody a tradition about Jesus, but this tradition has undergone many and important changes under the influence of this same life and faith. How far it is to be trusted as bringing us accurate information about his actual deeds and words can be determined, even approximately, only after the probable effects of early Christian beliefs and practices are taken fully into account. That authentic primitive memories are embodied in the Gospels, we will not deny; but the situation is that they must prove themselves to be such. The Gospels are primarily and prima facie church books, records of that complex of memory, experience, and belief which we call the primitive faith; and the burden of proof rests with any attempt to establish a particular item as historically accurate. The fact that in many cases this burden can easily be carried must not be allowed to obscure the fact that in every case it *must* be carried. With regard to our present theme it is indubitable that the early Church attributed the most momentous saving significance to Jesus' death. This is quite enough to account for ascriptions in the Gospels of similar views to Jesus himself. We shall be justified, therefore, in trusting the accuracy of these ascriptions only if the evidence for their authenticity is unmistakably clear—which usually means, in effect, only if the Church's ideas can themselves be naturally explained only on the assumption that Jesus held them first."

I have defined these positions perhaps more sharply than

is appropriate, and I would not claim that any scholar takes either position constantly and consistently. I am convinced, however, that every student of the Gospels is inclined to take one position or the other, and that his conclusions about any particular theme of the kind we now have before us are largely determined by which position he finds more congenial. It is for this reason, more than for any other, that equally competent scholars, with exactly the same evidence before them, can arrive at such different results. Thus, in the present case, some scholars ask, "What is to prevent our believing that Jesus is the creator of the conception of himself as the suffering Son of man?" And others ask, "What requires that we attribute to Jesus a conception which could so naturally have arisen out of the experience and reflection of the primitive Christians?" And the answer to each question is the same: "Nothing whatever." In other words, the position we take on the basic issue depends in no small part on which of these two questions we find it more natural to ask.

The point is probably obvious enough, but I should like to illustrate and enforce it still further by citing some sentences from a book of C. H. Dodd—sentences quoted with cordial approval by J. W. Bowman, whose own books would provide many passages of the same kind. Dodd writes:

The New Testament itself avers that it was Jesus Christ Himself who first directed the minds of His followers to certain parts of the scriptures as those in which they might find illumination upon the meaning of His mission and destiny. That He formally set before them a comprehensive scheme of biblical interpretation, after the manner of Lk. xxiv. 25-27, 44-45, we may well hesitate to believe; but I can see no reasonable ground for rejecting the statements of the Gospels that (for example) He pointed to Psalm cx as a better guide to the truth about His mission and destiny

39

than the popular beliefs about the Son of David, or that He made
that connection of the "Lord" at God's right hand with the Son
of Man in Daniel which proved so momentous for Christian
thought; or that He associated with the Son of Man language
which had been used of the Servant of the Lord, and employed it to
hint at the meaning, and the issue, of His own approaching death.
To account for the beginning of this most original and fruitful
process of rethinking the Old Testament we found need to postu-
late a creative mind. The Gospels offer us one. Are we compelled
to reject the offer? [2]

Note Dodd's phrases, "I can see no reasonable ground for
rejecting," and, even more clear in its implications, "Are we
compelled to reject?" Even where the negative case is admittedly very strong indeed, he does not "reject"; he only "hesi-
tates to believe." It is obvious that the burden of proof, as he
understands the situation, is carried by the negative.[3] But it
is just as plausible—I should say, much more plausible—to
ask the affirmative to bear this burden. Consider just one of
Dodd's instances, the use made of Ps. 110 in Mark 12:35-37:

And as Jesus taught in the temple, he said, "How can the scribes
say that the Christ is the son of David? David himself, inspired
by the Holy Spirit, declared,

'The Lord said to my Lord,

[2] *According to the Scriptures* (New York: Chas. Scribner's Sons, 1953; London:
Nisbet & Co., 1952), p. 110. Used by permission of the publishers. Quoted by
J. W. Bowman, *Prophetic Realism and the Gospel* (Philadelphia: Westminster
Press, 1955), p. 124.
[3] Another illustration of this same understanding or attitude is provided
by William Manson (*Jesus the Messiah* [Philadelphia: Westminster Press, 1946],
p. 165), when after a reference to the christological teaching of Phil. 2:8-9, he
asks: "Have we any right to say that such an expansion of ideas could have
arisen only after the crucifixion, and that it was not possible for Jesus in the
days of his flesh? To take this attitude may conceivably be to beg the whole
question of Christian origins." What I am trying to point out is that to put
the issue in just this way is in a sense already to have begged this same question.

Sit at my right hand,
till I put thy enemies under thy feet.'
David himself calls him Lord; so how is he his son?"

Here is a pericope obviously adapted to primitive Christian polemic and apologetic. Acts 2:34-35 and Heb. 1:13 indicate that it was so used. The materials for it lay manifestly at hand in the traditional scriptures. Do we need to go back of the early Church to find its original setting? Is it likely that there would have been any occasion for making this point about the relation of the Messiah to David until the need for establishing the messiahship of Jesus had arisen, and does not all the evidence indicate that this need did not arise until after the Resurrection? Even those who hold that Jesus toward the end of his career initiated his disciples into the secret of his messiahship must recognize that he forbade their making this fact known to others. Would Jesus himself, then, have been engaged in defending his messiahship against Jewish critics? If he was not defending or defining his own messianic role, he was carrying on a merely verbal exchange about a purely speculative question. But is this any more likely? In view of the impression of his mind and method which the Gospel accounts of Jesus' teaching as a whole make on us, is it not even less likely? In a word, is there any "reasonable ground for rejecting" (using Dodd's phrase but applying it in the obverse way) the obvious conclusion that this use of Ps. 110, which so aptly served the purposes of the early Church or some part of it, also had its origin in its life and thought? I should say that the same question can appropriately be asked of its use of Isa. 53.

III

Those who are inclined to find the origin of such uses in the reflection of the early Church rather than in the mind of Jesus are required to deal with at least three objections: First, it is objected that the early Church would not have ventured to attribute to Jesus sayings which he was not remembered to have uttered. Second, it is urged that these sayings, in particular those setting forth the theological significance of his life and death, presuppose too much originality and creative imagination to have been produced by the Church. And third, it is argued that even if it should be granted that the Church was willing and able to formulate such conceptions out of its own experience and thought, it could not have done so as early as the proposed theory of their origin requires.

As to the first objection—that the primitive Church would not have presumed to attribute to Jesus sayings which he was not remembered to have spoken—one needs only point to the indubitable fact that it actually did. Although the word "presumed" may not be appropriate in this connection, the Gospels unquestionably attribute words to Jesus which he never uttered. No critical student of the New Testament will deny that this is true of the Fourth Gospel, and to recognize the fact of such inventiveness in this Gospel is to acknowledge at least the possibility of it in the others. It is true that the Fourth Gospel appears as the work of some great individual—less a compilation of tradition than the other Gospels—and one may hesitate to ascribe this creative work to "the early Church." But this Gospel undoubtedly spoke for a community and out of its life, and not improbably embodied a tradition of some kind. Some students of the Dead Sea Scrolls are urging that this "Johannine" community and its tradition may be quite early. But no matter how early the community, or for that matter the Fourth Gospel itself, it is impossible, so long as we have the Synoptics, to attribute the discourses in that Gospel to Jesus himself. The words which it ascribes to Jesus are, for the greater part, concerned with the theological significance of Christ and are clearly attempts to formulate meanings which emerged only in and after the Resurrection. Indeed, the Christ of the Fourth Gospel is almost entirely preoccupied with his own significance to the complete neglect of the great themes of the righteous will, the abounding goodness, and the imminent kingdom of God which dominate and give their distinctive character to the utterances of Jesus in the other Gospels. But is there not every reason for assuming that the process of attributing to Jesus himself conceptions of his significance which had been wrought out in the life of the Church would have begun almost at once? And is it not therefore appropriate to ask those who deny the churchly origin of the scattered sayings of this same theologically pregnant kind in the Synoptic Gospels to bear the burden of proof?

It probably does not need to be added that the process we are discussing must not be thought of as involving intentional misrepresentation or moral cupability in any sense or degree. The distinction between what we call "the historical Jesus" and "the risen Christ" is much more real and important to us than it was for the Gospel writers or the communities for which they spoke. They would not have been as sharply aware of it, as much interested in it, or as much concerned to maintain it as we have become in our modern age. The important thing would have been what Christ had to say to the church and the world, not just when he said it, whether before his death or afterward. Besides, the efforts of early preachers and apologists to make the gospel vivid and relevant would inevitably have involved inventiveness of this kind. Indeed, in spite of the fact that for us the gospel has been given definite written form and has even been canonized, we still do not hesitate to create words for Jesus, not only in drama, novel, and poetry, but also in preaching. One who has not listened to preaching with this particular point in mind will be surprised by how often modern preachers (of course, without the slightest intention to mislead) put on Jesus' lips words which there is no record of his having spoken. Recorded sayings of Jesus are expanded—being interpreted and applied in ways which may be authentic enough (or may not be!) but for which there is certainly no explicit warrant in the tradition. In the primitive period, before the tradition had assumed either fixed or authoritative form, it was inevitable that some of these imaginatively created utterances should have become a part of it.

The second objection is more serious and requires more careful consideration—the objection that the christological statements attributed to Jesus are characterized by an originality, a creative power, which can only have belonged to Jesus himself. In particular, this is said of the synthesis of the Son of man and Suffering Servant conceptions. Here we have, to refer to the argument from Dodd already cited, what is probably the supreme example of a "most original process of rethinking the Old Testament." A "creative mind" is postulated. "The Gospels offer us one. Are we compelled to reject the offer?" John Wick Bowman asks where "originality generally [lies]—with the individual or with the community?" He answers: "Surely, experience is in favor of its lying with the individual." [4]

Now it is likely that such judgments underestimate the possibilities of group creativity—especially when the group is engaged in expressing or representing its own life. Of course in the obvious sense all thinking is done by individuals—a

[4] From *The Intention of Jesus* by John Wick Bowman, copyright, 1943, The Westminster Press, p. 86. Used by permission.

44

group as an essentially impersonal totality, almost an abstraction, does not think. But often an idea occurring in vague or incipient form to one member of a group so answers to and stimulates the minds of other members that, through the contributions of many, it gradually becomes a clear and fully developed conception. Every step in this process has been initiated in some individual mind, but the emergent conception can be described only as the product of a communal process. The idea that the prophetic picture of the Suffering Servant of the Lord, who went "like a lamb that is led to the slaughter," who "was wounded for our transgressions, . . . and with [whose] stripes we are healed"—the idea that this picture was fulfilled in the suffering and death of Jesus the Messiah must first have occurred, however tentatively and vaguely, to some individual; but so wonderfully would it have seemed to answer to the realities, both remembered and experiential, of the Church's life that, almost at once, its form would have become definite and clear and its truth self-evident and unquestionable.

But if such judgments as those of Dodd and Bowman underestimate the possibilities of this kind of communal thinking, they also exaggerate, it seems to me, the degree of originality involved in the working out of such a conception as this of the Servant-Messiah. They seem to imply that we are dealing here with a purely intellectual conception, a brilliant achievement of pure thought. But what we actually have is the utilization of a familiar and vivid image to express and explain a deeply felt concrete reality. Jesus was known as the Christ— he was actually present in the community as the Lord—and he was poignantly remembered to have suffered a terrible death. All of this was given, belonged to the essential substance of the Church's life. It was inevitable that the community (or or,,

individuals within it, if you prefer), constantly searching the scriptures for light on the meaning of the wonderful event, should seize on the image of the Suffering Servant in Isa. 53, especially as Jesus' whole life had been one of humble, self-sacrificing service and his death the death of an utterly innocent victim of human blindness and malice. I would not for a moment disparage the creative insight involved in this use of the Old Testament, but must not essentially the same kind of originality be attributed to those "black and unknown bards"[5] who in the spirituals utilized in manifestly authentic and often wonderfully moving ways various biblical themes in interpreting the experience of the Negro people? In both cases, familiar scriptures are being used to interpret a profoundly known reality. One does not need to ascribe the origin of such conceptions to brilliant thinking, much less to superhuman insight.

But, goes a third objection, even if it should be granted that the early Church was quite capable of arriving at the conception of Jesus as the suffering Son of man, could it have done so as early as that theory of the origin of the conception requires? Of course, there is ground for disagreement as to how early this must be presumed to have been. There is no question that before the end of the first century the messiahship of Jesus was being interpreted in the light of Isa. 53. First Clement, the Lucan writings, Matthew, I Peter, and Hebrews contain clear reminiscences of this chapter of Isaiah in interpreting the Passion. But many would dispute that Paul made any such use of it. Clarence T. Craig writes, "Paul shows an awareness of the chapter by a couple of quotations, but in neither case is there the slightest connection with vicarious suffering and

[5] From the title of a poem by James Weldon Johnson.

death." [6] Craig also denies that there is any convincing evidence of the influence of this passage upon Mark. Although I am sympathetic with Craig's thesis as a whole—namely, that Jesus did not regard himself as the Suffering Servant—I am not convinced by his argument with respect to Paul and Mark. Several passages in the Gospel, particularly 10:45 ("the Son of man came not to be ministered unto, but to minister, and to give his life a ransom for many"), seem to me most naturally to involve a reference to Isa. 53; and the same thing can be said, I think, of I Cor. 15:3 ("Christ died for our sins according to the scriptures"). I am inclined to agree with the majority of critics that the conception of Jesus the Messiah as the Suffering Servant has its origin in the pre-Pauline period. To say this, however, is not to say that the conception was put on Jesus' lips so early. There is no evidence that Jesus himself was being represented as identifying himself with the Suffering Servant (or for that matter with the Messiah-Son of man) until the time of Mark's Gospel, well after the middle of the first century.

Now as regards the emergence of the conception itself within a decade or less of the Resurrection I can see no difficulty. The necessity of interpreting the death of the Messiah would have lain heavily upon the first communities, and Isa. 53 was a readily available resource. The ascription of the idea to Jesus himself, however, raises another kind of problem. Is it possible that important utterances should have been created for Jesus and become embodied in the tradition as his own at a time when eyewitnesses were still living and presumably in positions of influence and leadership in the Church? This question does not arise so acutely in connection with the Servant-Messiah

[6] "Jesus and the Suffering Servant," *Journal of Religion*, XXIV (October, 1944), 240-46.

47

sayings of Jesus, for these, as we have just seen, do not need to be dated earlier than, say, A.D. 70, when eyewitness testimony may no longer have been available. It is often a quite pertinent query, however: as, for example, in connection with the words of Jesus at the Last Supper—words which, as they stand in Paul and therefore as early as A.D. 50, clearly attribute a vicarious sacrificial significance to Christ's death. Jeremias [7] with great persuasiveness argues for a somewhat simpler form of words (but still words strongly suggesting a sacrificial meaning) lying back of both Paul and the Gospels and therefore traceable to a date hardly more than a decade after the Crucifixion. One is forced to ask then: Is it possible that as early as this it could have been repeated over and over again in the recurrent celebrations of the Lord's Supper that Jesus said, "This is my body" and "This is my blood," if in fact he had not done so?

The question is a searching one; and it is quite possible, even likely, that in this case we should decide that the words, or some such words, were actually spoken.[8] Still, to the general question as asked—the question whether it is conceivable that within as short a time as a single decade words were being attributed to Jesus which he did not speak—to this question

[7] *Op. cit.*, pp. 72-135.

[8] I say "some such words" because of the grave difficulties involved in our thinking of a Palestinian Jew as speaking, even symbolically, of the drinking of blood. Perhaps the context of Jesus' words (whatever they were exactly) was quite different from that in which they stand in the tradition. Is it not possible that Jesus made some allusion to bread and wine as symbols of his death, but without the suggestion that his body was to be eaten or his blood to be drunk? Many would hold that Paul's account of Jesus' words in connection with the cup is more primitive just because it avoids any suggestion of an actual drinking of blood. (But see Jeremias, *op. cit.*, pp. 134-35.) This is a large and complicated subject, and I am not presuming to go into it. My point here is only to concede the probability that something happened in Jesus' last supper with his disciples—something involving words and actions of Jesus—which provided the basis for the later Eucharist.

I believe the answer has to be Yes. As a case in point, I may refer again to the saying in Mark 12:35 ff. about the meaning of Ps. 110. Now this saying, as we have seen, bears every mark of being the creation of the early Church. But if so, it must be very primitive indeed, for it seems to be a defense of the messiahship of Jesus based on a common acknowledgment of his non-Davidic descent. But certainly as early as Paul's letter to the Romans (see Rom. 1:3), and probably much earlier, Jesus' Davidic ancestry was being affirmed.

In general, it must be recognized that whereas eyewitness testimony would always have exercised a decisive check upon *denials* of what Jesus said or did—for example, it would have prevented a denial of Jesus' baptism by John—such testimony would have been much less influential in preventing the *creation* of either words or incidents. The eyewitness could affirm what he remembered; he could not deny what was "remembered" by another. Indeed, if the item thus "remembered" was such as to clarify and support his own faith, he not only would have had no interest in denying it; he would have had every reason for accepting it gladly and confidently.

IV

Still one other matter of a general kind needs to be considered before we turn in the next chapter more directly to the question of fact as to how Jesus thought of himself and his death. This is the question of how important this issue of "Jesus or the early Church" is. The principal fault I find with the admirable book of J. W. Bowman *The Intention of Jesus* is that he seems to me grossly to exaggerate this importance with respect to the very matter we are considering in these chapters. He writes:

The *voice* of Old Testament prophecy proclaimed the advent of two great personalities—a *Remnant-Messiah* and a *Suffering Servant of the Lord*. . . . The "Suffering Servant" is the fruitage of the Deutero-Isaiah's inspired meditation; the "Remnant-Messiah" idea was a slower growth. . . . But *who first brought these terms together into a fertilizing union?* This question is of cosmic significance. The answer to it is the name of the originator of Christianity as we know it. He is the creator of the New Testament faith and of the Christian Church.

Later he adds: "To say that the Church produced the faith by which it lives is to affirm the possibility of an ethicospiritual perpetual-motion machine!" [9]

Now such words seem to say that the origin of Christianity lay in an idea—or in a combination of two ideas—when actually it lay in something far more objective and real, in an actual event. There can be no doubt as to who is "the creator of the New Testament faith and of the New Testament church" if either has the truth and importance Christians affirm. That creator is neither Jesus nor the Church, but is God. No question, such as this, about who first entertained a given conception can have "cosmic significance," as though the truth of an idea depended on who first thought of it, or as though the Church, for that matter, sprang from an idea at all. The truth of the conception depends only on how well it answers to the concrete reality to which it applies, and its importance depends only upon how important that same reality is. To say that the Church developed this or that phrase or set of terms for the formulation of its faith is by no means to say that it "produced the faith by which it lives" in the manner of a "perpetual motion machine." The faith of the early

[9] *Op. cit.*, pp. 81, 82, 86.

Church was one phase of a creative event which involved many elements, actual and ideal; and the Creator of that event, as of all creative events, was no one participant in it, whether individual or community, nor was it all of the participants together, but was the God of history himself.

I have earlier ventured the opinion that it is unnecessary to attribute a great deal of originality to whatever individual or community first utilized the image of the Suffering Servant to interpret the death of Jesus the Christ. But this does not mean that something wonderfully "original" and mightily creative did not occur in first-century Palestine. This was the event in which the whole experience of Israel, the personality of Jesus, the responses he evoked, the words he spoke, the incidents in his career, his death, his resurrection, the Church and its faith, all participate and in which they are all bound or fused into an indissoluble organic whole. But need it be asked who is the author of this "creative synthesis"? And when the answer to that question is clearly seen, can it seem very important to whom this conception of the suffering Messiah, or any other conception for that matter, first occurred?

CHAPTER THREE

The Psychological Question

WE HAVE SEEN THAT THE PROBLEM WHETHER JESUS ATTRIBUTED
the kind of theological significance to his death which the
Church has always found in it is bound up with the question
whether he thought of himself as the Servant-Messiah, and that
how we answer this question depends less perhaps on how we
look at particular pieces of evidence in the Gospels than on
the point of view from which we look at the Gospel evidence
as a whole. Our answer depends, it has been argued, on where
we are disposed to place the burden of proof—whether on
those who regard any particular saying attributed to Jesus as
having been literally his own, as being "authentic" in this
narrow sense, or on those who ascribe it to the primitive
Church. There are many sayings in the Gospels which virtually
all scholars acknowledge as being in all probability Jesus' own.
There are others which all agree could hardly have been spoken
by him. But there remain not a few—and these include many
of the sayings most pertinent to our inquiry—concerning whose
"authenticity" the scholars differ; and this difference, I am
saying, is in large part a reflection of the difference in point
of view to which I am referring. Those who assume that these
sayings need to be disproved are almost bound to accept them;
those who feel that they must be proved are equally likely to
reject them.

Now I cannot pretend to have transcended this difference. In the preceding chapter I was attempting to present the issue itself, but I made no effort to conceal my own position. Although I do not need, more than others, to confess to the fault of consistency, nevertheless it will be clear that I tend to take the second position and to emphasize the creative role of the primitive Church, especially when sayings of Jesus about himself are under consideration. The fact that the Gospels as they come to us are actually productions of the early Church; the fact that when, with the Resurrection, the Church was fully in existence, it would have found itself under immediate and growing pressure to understand and interpret, in the light of the meaning it had proved to have, the whole event of which the death of Jesus had been so important a part; the fact that the materials of the Servant-Messiah conception of Jesus' nature and role lay readily at hand; the fact that once the Church thought of him so, it was inevitable that it should soon ascribe the same thoughts to Jesus himself—these facts, it seems to me, make it appropriate that those who find the origin of the conception in Jesus' own mind should bear the burden of proof. After all, we ourselves find it very hard, as we were observing at the beginning of the preceding chapter, to suppose that Jesus could have had different thoughts about himself and his death than we have come to accept as true ourselves. That same difficulty would have been felt also by the first believers; and if for us, in our modern critical age, it can often be a serious stumbling block, for them it would have been a quite insuperable obstacle. In a word, since the Church would almost inevitably have represented Jesus as being consciously the Servant-Messiah, whether that was actually true or not, we are justified in asking that the evidence of his having entertained such a conception about himself should be unmistakably strong and clear.

I

Now this evidence must be looked at in the light of still another fact of a general or prior sort which would seem to challenge the traditional position on this issue and increase the burden of proof which those who maintain that position must carry. I am referring to the psychological implausibility of the conception of the Servant-Messiah as a mode of Jesus' own self-consciousness. We have seen that this idea can be easily thought of as originating in the reflection of the early Church—it answers in a remarkable way to the event as it was remembered and as its meaning had become known in the Church's life. Not only is there no psychological improbability in the Church's having developed the conception; that development seems so natural as to appear almost inevitable. But the case is quite different when the origin of the conception is found in Jesus' own mind. Those who take that view encounter psychological difficulties of a grave kind which, in my judgment, they often do not take seriously enough or adequately deal with.

These difficulties would be less grave if it were not for the particular form which Jesus' conception of the "Messiah," if it conformed to any current type of expectation, must be thought of as taking. Now few things about the picture of Jewish messianic speculation in the first century are so clear as that the picture itself is not clear at all, and it may seem rash to speak of "any current type of expectation" when our knowledge of the possibilities is so limited. The messianic hope was a lush growth manifesting an almost endless variety of forms. It would appear that many Jews who expected the kingdom of God did not associate it with any messianic figure—that is, the coming Kingdom would be God's alone, and he would make use of no single or supreme agent, whether human or divine, in establishing it.[1] But more prevalent, apparently, was the belief that God would act through, or in close connection with, an "anointed" person, a divinely chosen and endowed leader of the people. The term "the Messiah" only gradually came into use, and one can be certain of its prevalence only late (perhaps only shortly before Jesus' own time), but the essential sense of the term was undoubtedly present long before. The Messiah was most often thought of as a warrior or king, a "son of David"—really a David redivivus [2]—but he could also be conceived of as a "Prophet . . . like unto [Moses]" (Deut. 18:15-19), or as Elijah returning (Mal. 3:1-5; 4: 1-6), or again as a great high priest.[3] These conceptions tended to run together, and the possible combinations and mutual transmutations among them are obviously almost without limit. There is good reason to believe that the "king" motif was the dominant one; but the Messiah-King might also be the prophet, or the priest, or both. Some students of the Dead Sea Scrolls find in the phrase "the anointed ones of Aaron and Israel" [4] evidence that the Qumran community

[1] Among sources which appear to reflect such a purely theocratic conception may be mentioned Amos, Zephaniah, Nahum, Habakkuk, Joel, the Books of Maccabees, I Baruch, I Enoch 1-36 and 91-104, and others.

[2] As, for example, in Isa. 9:2-7 and 11:1-9; Jer. 23:1-6 and 33:15-17; Ezek. 34:23-31 and 37:21-28; The Testaments of the Twelve Patriarchs: Judah 24:5-6; Psalms of Solomon 17:23 ff.

[3] Ps. 110; I Macc. 14:27 ff.; The Testaments of the Twelve Patriarchs: Levi 8:14-15; 18:2 ff. See also William H. Brownlee. "Messianic Motifs of Qumran and the Testament," *New Testament Studies*, III, 195 ff.

[4] The *Manual of Discipline.* But the "Damascus Document" speaks of "the Messiah of Aaron and Israel" (9:10). But see K. G. Kuhn, "The Two Messiahs of Aaron and Israel," in K. Stendahl (ed.), *The Scrolls and the New Testament* (New York: Harper & Brothers, 1957), pp. 54-64. Kuhn is convinced that among the Essenes two Messiahs were expected, the Messiah of Aaron having

expected two "Messiahs," a king and a priest, or (since a prophet is spoken of also in the same connection) even three. Whether each or any of these, despite the use of the word "anointed," was thought of as "the Messiah" in the full sense seems open to some question. Further discovery and study will doubtless clarify the picture. But whatever conclusion is finally reached on this point, the scrolls will continue to bear witness to the exuberance and variety characteristic of messianic speculation in the Palestine of the first century.

Thus far the picture is very confused indeed. But over against all of these conceptions of the Messiah stands another conception, which can be distinguished from them all much more clearly than they can be distinguished from one another. This was the conception of the Son of man—a heavenly being who would be revealed in the last times as God's agent in judgment and redemption. The phrase "son of man" could mean simply man (it is so used in Ezekiel and elsewhere in the Old Testament) and is likely to mislead modern readers by suggesting that when applied to the "coming one," it is his *humanity* which must be especially in view. Actually almost precisely the opposite is the case. Over against the several types of basically human messiahs stands this divine Son of man. So far as we know, it is Daniel who first "sees" his form in apocalyptic vision. After the appearance of the several beasts representing the alien empires to which Israel had been subject, the last of them being Syria, under whose tyrannical dominion she was then suffering—after this Daniel saw "one like unto a son of man." This heavenly man, to whom the "kingdom" is given, obviously stands for Israel in Daniel's apocalypse and may be no more than a symbol for the nation. But in the Similitudes

---

precedence. He accounts for the singular "Messiah" in the Damascus Document by later scribal emendation.

of Enoch and in II Esdras he is clearly thought of as a heavenly person, an angel-like being closest of all to "the Lord of spirits," and the one to whom the "messianic" functions of final judgment and redemption have been committed.[5]

Now the psychological difficulty involved in the view that Jesus considered himself to be the Messiah is as grave as it is because it requires that we think of him as identifying himself, not as the Messiah in any of the several basically human senses we have mentioned, but as this Son of man. His conception of God's agent in the coming crisis, if he had a conception of this kind at all, was not the traditional one of the human being whom God would choose, endow, and exalt to the office of Messiah, whether conceived of in kingly, priestly, or prophetic terms, or in terms of some combination of these conceptions, but rather took the form of a supernatural being who at the appointed time would appear on the clouds of heaven. The evidence for this conclusion will be more fully stated in the next chapter. The principal and really decisive item in it is the striking paucity in Jesus' recorded teachings of references to the Messiah as compared with the allusions to the Son of man. Only about thirteen times is Jesus represented as mentioning the "Messiah" (or the "Christ" or the "King"); but the "Son of man" (in some sense of that term) is found almost seventy times on Jesus' lips. Since the earliest Christian communities among which the gospel tradition began to take fixed form were convinced that Jesus was the Messiah and habitually used that term to express their faith, the very occasional ascriptions of its use to Jesus himself can be plausibly explained as representing a development in the Church's tradition. Since Jesus *was* the Messiah, it would have been argued, he must have known and spoken about him. But Jesus' refer-

[5] See Dan. 7:13-14; Enoch 39:3-6; 46:1-8; 48:1-10; 52:1-9; II Esdras 13:1-53.

ences to "the Son of man" resist this kind of explanation, not only because of their greater number, but also because of the absence of evidence that the primitive Church, or any part of it, was accustomed to use the term in expressing its own faith. Now other Jews of Jesus' own general period are known to have entertained messianic pretentions; and if there were strong evidence that Jesus thought of himself as Messiah, whether as "son of David," or "one like unto Moses," or in any other similar way, there would be no a priori obstacle to our accepting that conclusion. Actually, however, there is every reason to believe, not only that Jesus did not think of himself in this way, but also that he did not think in strictly messianic terms at all. If he identified himself with any figure in contemporary Jewish speculation about the coming kingdom of God, it was not with the human Messiah, but with the divine Son of man.[6]

II

But such self-identification, it seems to me, involves the most serious psychological difficulties. Could so sane a person have entertained such thoughts about himself? How could such a person have identified himself with the essentially super-human personage of the apocalypses—with him who, "sitting at the right hand of Power," will come "with the clouds of heaven" (Mark 14:62)?[7] Attempts to answer this question

---

[6] As I have said, the evidence for this view will be presented in the next chapter. Meantime, it may be said that few scholars would question the assertion that Jesus found the term "Son of man" more congenial than "Messiah" whether he is thought of as applying it to himself or not.

[7] Both in Daniel and in II Esdras the Son of man is spoken of as "coming [or 'flying'] with the clouds of heaven." It has been argued (notably by T. F. Glasson in *The Second Advent* [London: Epworth Press, 1945], pp. 63-68) that the "coming" was toward heaven and not toward earth, and that what is being spoken of is the exaltation or enthronement of the Son of man rather than his

have taken several forms. Rudolf Otto [8] bases on a disputed text in the Similitudes of Enoch the view that there was current in Jesus' time the conception of a human being who was later to become the divine Son of man, and that therefore Jesus' self-identification is not as strange and anomalous as it might at first appear. Jesus means that he will be vindicated as the Son of man when the imminent Kingdom comes and is now the Son of man only in an anticipatory or proleptic sense. But the element of apparent pretension in the claim that one will "become" the Son of man is almost if not quite as great as in the claim that one *is* that personage. Besides, there is an important difference between supposing that a particular human being (for example, Enoch) had proved to be the Son of man and maintaining such an identity in one's own case. Otto's hypothesis, although it may if true slightly mitigate the strangeness, certainly does not remove it.

T. W. Manson has proposed that Jesus' use of the phrase "Son of man" harks back, not to II Esdras or the Similitudes of Enoch (the works in which the apocalyptic notion appears most clearly) or to some community for which these books

---

messianic Parousia. Some support for this understanding can certainly be found in Daniel (7:13), but hardly elsewhere. As H. K. McArthur has shown in a paper read before the Society of Biblical Literature, even this passage was not thought of as having this meaning once it came to be interpreted messianically. McArthur also makes the point that in Mark 14:62 the order of the two crucial phrases indicates that the idea of Parousia is paramount. Otherwise the saying would be: ". . . coming with the clouds of heaven and seated at the right hand of Power." Actually, however, if it is supposed that Jesus is speaking of himself in this passage, the psychological difficulties we are discussing are as great if Mark 14:62 is taken in the one way as in the other.

[8] *The Kingdom of God and the Son of Man,* tr. F. V. Filson and B. L. Woolf (Grand Rapids, Mich.: Zondervan Publishing House, 1938), pp. 201-18. On the question of the identification of Enoch with the Son of man of the parables of Enoch see E. Sjöberg, *Der Menschensohn im Äthiopischen Henochbuch* (Lund: C. W. K. Gleerup, 1946), pp. 147-89. Sjöberg strongly affirms the fact of the identification.

or some of their sources spoke, but rather to the book of Daniel, in which "the Son of Man is, like the Servant of Jehovah, an ideal figure and stands for the manifestation of the Kingdom of God on earth in a people wholly devoted to their heavenly King." [9] Manson interprets Jesus' purpose as being "to create the Son of Man, the Kingdom of the saints of the Most High, to realise in Israel the ideal contained in the term." He continues:

This task is attempted in two ways: first by public appeal . . . : then, when this appeal produced no adequate response, by the consolidation of his own band of followers. Finally, when it becomes apparent that not even the disciples are ready to rise to the demands of the ideal, he stands alone, embodying in his own person the perfect human response to the regal claims of God.[10]

George S. Duncan, whose book *Jesus, Son of Man* deserves much more attention than it seems to have received, while respectful to the suggestion of Manson and inclined to agree that Daniel is a more likely source of Jesus' conception than Enoch, nevertheless finds it inadequate.

Not all of the uses of the phrase "the Son of Man" [he writes (I should say "not many")] admit of this interpretation, and Dr. Manson is driven to explain some of these as due to a misunderstanding of the original. Is it likely, we may ask, that Daniel's simile, "one like a son of man," is by itself an adequate explanation of a concept which so thoroughly dominated the outlook and

[9] *The Teaching of Jesus* (London: Cambridge University Press, 1931), p. 227. Used by permission of the publisher.

[10] *Ibid.*, pp. 227-28. Manson has modified his position somewhat in more recent writing, but not I think in such a way as to make the quotation of these sentences less apt in the present connection. See his "The Son of Man in Daniel, Enoch, and the Gospels," *Bulletin of the John Rylands Library* 32. 2 and *The Servant-Messiah* (London: Cambridge University Press, 1953), pp. 72 ff.

teaching of Jesus? And is it natural that a phrase, which by its very nature has primarily an individual reference, should have been made by Jesus (apparently without explanation) to refer in the first instance to a people, and have only later, and in a derived sense, been made to refer to Himself as the individual and unique representative of that people.[11]

The improbability of such a development seems even greater when we consider that the term "Son of man" had already come to have, in certain influential quarters at least, an *accepted, but quite different, individual significance,* and moreover that many of the most striking uses of the term by Jesus conform exactly to this accepted pattern. If one attributes all the Gospel instances of the "Son of man" which do not suit Manson's conception to "misunderstanding," one might as well go only a little further and deny that Jesus used the phrase as a title at all.

Duncan's own conception of Jesus' meaning when he identified himself with the Son of man is quite different. Beginning by recognizing that

in the faith of Israel . . . man has a central place in the purposes of God . . . ; [that he] is the most precious of all God's creatures . . . marked out for a position of lordship; and in the main it is through man that God's purposes for His creation are to be advanced . . . [that redeemed from the consequences of his rebellion] man will be reinstated in the position of power which God meant him to have in the universe, and through him God's sovereign sway will be extended throughout all creation

[11] (New York: The Macmillan Co., 1949), p. 143. Used by permission of the publisher. See also the telling criticism of Manson's view in Vincent Taylor, *Jesus and His Sacrifice* (London: Macmillan & Co., 1937), pp. 24 ff., and Sjöberg, *Der verborgene Menschensohn in den Evangelien* (Lund: C. W. K. Gleerup, 1955), p. 241.

—beginning here, Duncan goes on to say: "Thus, while in some quarters the thought of the triumph of God found definite expression in the expectation of a Messiah, in others it would seem to have expressed itself more generally in the expectation of a Man in whom God's purposes for mankind and for the world should be fulfilled." [12] Duncan is alluding, not to the conception of the apocalyptic Son of man from heaven, nor yet to any prevalent near Eastern conception of the primordial, archetypal Man,[13] but to a man who was destined to become *the* Man. As Duncan understands the Gospels, Jesus was identifying himself with that perfect and unique Man, who in the last days was to appear as the Savior of the world.

A number of questions about this proposal are likely to occur to us. For one thing, do the actual occurrences of the phrase "Son of man" in the Gospels, taken as a whole, fit this view better than they do Manson's? For another, what is the evidence for the existence of the kind of eschatological expectation Duncan refers to—this "Man in whom God's purposes for mankind and for the world should be fulfilled"? We have some such conception in Paul, to be sure, although there is no evidence that it was identical with or derived from the Son of man conception in the Synoptics. But in any case this was after the event. The only evidence Duncan cites for his view is the use of the phrase in Ezekiel:

In the opening vision we see how the prophet, realising his insignificance as a child of man in presence of the glory of the Most High, falls down upon his face; but, being summoned by God to stand upon his feet, he becomes possessed with the Spirit of God, he listens devoutly to what God has to say to him, and

[12] *Ibid.,* p. 144.
[13] Such as Carl Kraeling discusses in *Anthropos and Son of Man* (New York: Columbia University Press, 1927).

then he is sent forth to proclaim the divine message to his brethren. Thus his "manhood" is turned by God from weakness into strength, from insignificance into dignity with accompanying responsibility; he becomes a prophet of God, a chosen vessel for the transmission of the divine Word and Spirit. There is moreover this other facet to his manhood, that when he addresses himself to his prophetic mission he is not merely an Israelite speaking to Israel, he is a "son of man" proclaiming how the children of men in every nation, in Babylon, Tyre and Egypt no less than in Israel, are subject to the jurisdiction of the Lord of Hosts.

Duncan concludes:

It is in the light of Ezekiel's reminders of the way in which God deals with man—lifting him up from the ground, making known to him His will, filling him with His Spirit, and commissioning him to be His servant for the establishment of His kingdom throughout His whole creation—that we ought to seek to interpret the thoughts of Jesus regarding the Son of Man.[14]

I have quoted Duncan at length because it seems to me there is at least a possibility that if Jesus referred to himself as the Son of man, he was in some degree influenced by Ezekiel. There is no evidence, however, that Ezekiel thought of himself as "the Man" or even of his expecting the appearance of such a person.

But such suggestions as those of Otto, Manson, and Duncan, even if one or another of them should be found acceptable, would mitigate only slightly the psychological difficulties we are discussing. The basic problem remains: Would it be psychologically possible for a sane person to think of himself as either the Enochian Son of man, the Danielic Son of man,

[14] *Op. cit.*, pp. 145-46. See also W. A. Curtis, *Jesus Christ the Teacher* (London: Oxford University Press, 1943), pp. 127-43.

63

or "the Man" in what I should be inclined to call the later Pauline sense? This question is scarcely susceptible of a verifiable answer. It calls necessarily for a subjective judgment. All one has a right to ask is that it be fully and seriously considered. For myself, I find it exceedingly hard to answer it affirmatively.

Leaving out the account the implausibilities which are associated with the apocalyptic meanings of "Son of man"—the implausibilities which Otto, Manson, and Duncan are concerned to mitigate but which none of them, even if right, entirely removes—one is still left with enormous difficulties of a more basic kind. All of the proposals we have discussed involve ascribing to Jesus a unique consciousness of virtue—more than that, a consciousness of unique virtue. T. W. Manson writes: "Finally, . . . he stands alone, embodying in his own person the perfect human response to the regal claims of God." [15] The point, it must be noted, is not that he *did* embody this response—this point might be granted—but that he was conscious of doing so. Duncan speaks of Jesus' knowing that "in all Israel" he was the only one in "whose life the Father could recognise the spirit of Sonship." [16] And again it must be pointed out that the affirmation is not that he *was* thus unique but that he thought of himself as being so. John Wick Bowman can write: "Jesus knew himself to be the Messiah because of the great love for men that welled up within his soul: he knew himself to be the Messiah because he knew he possessed the only character that could make one worthy—he was man's utter Lover." [17] This sentence of Bowman's is especially unfortunate because it suggests that Jesus' belief in his messiahship was, not a matter of immediate and intuitive awareness, but

[15] *Op. cit.,* p. 228.
[16] *Op. cit.,* p. 115.
[17] *The Intention of Jesus,* pp. 180-81. See also pp. 145, 152.

an inference drawn from the perfection of his own character. "Must I not be the Messiah," Jesus seems to be saying to himself, "since I am possessed of such amazing goodness?" But I find, not Bowman's alone, but all of these statements unacceptable—not only because they seem to reflect, paradoxically enough, upon the moral character of Jesus as that character appears in the Gospels as a whole, but also because they are psychologically incredible. A sane person, not to say a good person, just could not think of himself in such a way.

III

The difficulty we are discussing appears in a special and, I should say, a particularly acute form in a book by Oscar Cullmann, to which reference has already been made, *The State in the New Testament*. His discussion of Jesus and the Zealots, in the course of which he presents impressive evidence that Zealots belonged to Jesus' following and that "his appearance with his disciples could have been mistaken for Zealotism," reaches its climax in the assertion that even

for Jesus [himself] the Zealot ideal constituted the true temptation —from the very beginning, when the devil offered him world dominion after his baptism, to the moment when he rebuked Peter as Satan, and finally to the decisive moment in Gethsemane, when the devil once again tempted him in the same way as in the beginning. . . . There in Gethsemane for the last time the question is posed, whether Jesus will yield to the pressure of his disciples and offer resistance to the Roman soldiers who have come to arrest him.[18]

This proposal of Cullmann's (that Zealotism was always a kind of "live option" for Jesus, a real temptation) is repeated later in the same book:

[18] *Op. cit.*, pp. 17-18. Used by permission of Chas. Scribner's Sons.

Christ regarded as expressly satanic the understanding of the Messiah which was advocated by the Zealots and which involved a confusion of the Kingdom of God with an earthly form of the State aimed at world domination. And truly one is tempted only by the things which stand near him.

Cullmann then goes on to say:

Thus the question of messianic consciousness is raised. . . . We wish only to indicate the point which is basic to the understanding both of Jesus' attitude and also of his condemnation: namely, that Jesus regarded himself as the Son of Man who would one day come on the clouds of heaven. . . . To be sure, the genuine Jewish Messiah is a victorious national commander-in-chief who conquers all heathen peoples and rules over the world; whereas the Danielic Son of Man comes from heaven and establishes a kingdom which is not of this world. But the connections between Messiah and Son of Man are of such a sort that we can properly speak of Jesus' messianic consciousness. Jesus was conscious of being the divine emissary, sent to establish the Kingdom of God. Only thus do we understand how Jesus became liable to the indictment which ended in his condemnation, the grounds for which were posted publicly on the cross. Jesus' guilt, from the Roman point of view, consisted in this: that—just like the Zealots—he was presumed to have aimed at kingly authority in one of the subject provinces of the Romans. Jesus' condemnation by the Romans . . . would be incomprehensible if Jesus had not in fact regarded himself as the Son of Man who came to establish the Kingdom of God in the world.[19]

I find here a serious *non sequitur*. Are we to have such confidence in juridical processes in general, and in those of Roman provincial government in particular, as to assume that Jesus

[19] *Ibid.*, pp. 24-26.

could not have been indicted and crucified for a "crime" of which he was entirely innocent? That he was a *supposed* claimant to kingship is clear and sure; that he must, therefore, have been a *real* claimant to kingship (in whatever sense) does not follow at all.

But what I have particularly in mind in citing these passages at this stage of our discussion is not this *non sequitur,* but rather the difficulty of seeing how Jesus could have been both aware of himself as "the Son of Man who would one day come on the clouds of heaven" to establish "a kingdom which is not of this world" and at the same time recurrently or constantly under temptation to head a Zealot movement to overthrow the state by force of arms. What kind of mentality are we attributing to Jesus when we make him subject to this kind of conflict and division? It might be plausibly argued that Jesus, under great pressure from Zealot followers and from the Zealot-minded populace, was under continual or frequent temptation to become a "national commander in chief." Although we may not find this argument convincing—and I do not—still we must recognize that the Gospels offer some evidence to support it and also that the state of mind which it ascribes to Jesus is understandable from both a historical and a psychological point of view. But when we further claim that this same person was firmly aware of himself as being the divine Son of man who would soon "come on the clouds of heaven," are we not forcing him into an almost impossible psychological mold? Admittedly these paragraphs from Cullmann raise this question in an acute form, but they only accentuate the difficulty of any view which attributes to Jesus an identification of himself with the Son of man of the apocalypses. We repeat our conclusion that a sane man could hardly have entertained such thoughts about himself.

IV

Two objections to this negative conclusion may be urged. The first is that it involves a modernization of Jesus. We are reminded that Jesus was an ancient Jew, that his thought world was very different from ours, that it was possible for him to entertain conceptions which are bound to seem to us strange or even repellent. All of this is true. These differences between Jesus' age and ours are real and important, and we often ignore them. The question remains, however, whether the psychological implausibilities we have been discussing are not so gross that even the widest differences in culture would be, in the last resort, irrelevant. It would seem to me that they are. Can we cite a really analogous case? Although we cannot be sure yet, it seems quite unlikely that the Dead Sea Scrolls will furnish us with one; [20] and neither I nor more learned friends whom I have consulted about this have been able to suggest one out of other extant Jewish literature. What may seem to the modern person to be extravagant, *prophetic* claims can certainly be found. Even messianic claims were sometimes made (although, as we shall see, not as often perhaps as is sometimes supposed) and were sufficiently plausible to be believed and supported by thousands. But are there other instances of a sane Jew's identifying himself with a divine being seated (or to be seated) at the right hand of God and coming with the clouds of heaven? To be sure, Simon Magus (Acts 8:9 ff.), a Samaritan, is described as thinking he was

[20] One is bound to think here of some of the Thanksgiving psalms. If the "I" in these psalms represents the Teacher of Righteousness or some other individual, then we must say that he is able to think and to speak about himself in terms which are very "high" indeed. But there is no sign of the heavenly Son of man. And there is always the possibility that the singular first personal pronoun, as in many of the canonical psalms, stands for the consecrated community, the people of God.

"somebody great" and as causing people to say about him, "This man is that power of God which is called Great." In other words, there were "possessed persons"; and the person possessed could sometimes be identified with the power which possessed him—perhaps could identify himself so. Just as in Mark 5:9 a demoniac could say to Jesus, "My name is Legion; for we are many," so the divinely possessed person of whatever kind may find his own personality lost in, or displaced by, that of the supernatural possessing power. But do we have knowledge of even such a one's claiming to be the Son of man? [21] And if, with T. W. Manson and others, one understands Jesus' use of the title in a nonapocalyptic sense—as standing for his consciousness of being the only true member of the people of God—must it not be said that a really good or saintly man who was conscious of himself as being such would seem impossible in any age?

"But," goes the second objection, "Jesus was more than a man. You are treating his case as though we were dealing with another human being like ourselves, but that is not true and makes all the difference. The criteria of mental health and of goodness which apply in other cases do not apply in his." I do not want to get involved in any discussion of Jesus' "nature" (which, I should say, is and must remain as deep a mystery to us as is the ultimate and essential nature of everything else in God's creation). But for our present purposes we do not need to proceed very far in that direction or to settle upon a definition of the "person" of Jesus. The issue just here is, not whether or in what sense Jesus was "more than a

[21] Of course, such a claim might conceivably have been made. But would we not regard it, if sincere, as a sign of mental illness? In any case, few would hold that the evidence permits of our thinking of Jesus as an "ecstatic" in this pathological, or near-pathological, sense. On "possession" see further below, pp. 114-15.

man," but whether he was a man at all. And this issue, the issue of his authentic humanity, is, I should say, more important, devotionally and theologically, than any other question one may ask about his "nature." Unless it be agreed that he was "truly man," it does not greatly matter what else can be said of him, because he will have been effectually separated from us and from our history. But the authentic marks of Jesus' humanity are not found in his physical appearance or in his susceptibility to hunger, thirst, or weariness; types of Docetism could acknowledge all of these. The really authentic marks must be found in his consciousness. Unless he had a human consciousness, he was not a man. If he did not think and feel, about himself and others, as a man does; if he did not take man's lot for granted as being intimately, entirely, and irrevocably his own; if he did not share, at the very deepest levels of his conscious and subconscious life, in our human anxieties, perplexities, and loneliness; if his joys were not characteristic human joys and his hopes, human hopes; if his knowledge of God was not in every part and under every aspect the kind of knowledge which it is given to man, the creature, to have—then he was not a true human being, he was not made man, and the Docetists were essentially right. If by being "more than a man" we mean that he lacked the normal self-consciousness of a man, then we are saying that he was less than a man. We are rejecting his humanity at the really decisive point. It may be possible to think of him as being "more than a man" in ways which permit us to think of him also as being a man, but we cannot think of him as *knowing* he was more than man without denying that he was man at all—that is, a true, sane man.

Now we cannot avoid relying on subjective impressions in dealing with this second objection, as with the first; but I,

70

for one, simply cannot imagine a sane human being, of any historical period or culture, entertaining the thoughts about himself which the Gospels, as they stand, often attribute to him or even the thoughts which the modern critical scholars who have been cited can suppose him to have had.

A well-known contemporary New Testament scholar, commenting on a colleague's remark that it was difficult to see how Jesus could in all sanity have thought of himself as being the apocalyptic Son of man, asked, "But suppose he *was* the Son of man?" Now I find such a question very hard to deal with, not because of what it asks for, but because of what it seems to presuppose. It seems to ascribe to the "Son of man" objective and personal reality. It seems to assume that there was, and is, a Son of man. But what does the phrase "Son of man," in the context of apocalypticism (and no one can deny that context in many of the Gospel statements), really designate? Must we not say that it stands for an idea, or an image, in the minds of certain ancient Jews? One can trace to some extent the beginnings and development of this idea or image in Jewish culture. But do we for a moment suppose that it is the name of any actual person—that the Son of man in fact exists or ever existed? If Jesus expected the coming of the apocalyptic Son of man, then are we not forced to say that he was, so far as we can see, mistaken? And if we are convinced that he went further and actually identified himself with the figure of the Coming One, are we not attributing to him an even deeper error? One may argue that in Jesus' place and time such self-deception was compatible with sanity (although I wonder again if a really comparable case can be found)—but that does not make it any the less truly self-deception. If Jesus was divine in a way to make psychologically plausible his consciousness of being the apocalyptic Son of man, one

71

would suppose that he would also have been divinely aware that there was no apocalyptic Son of man.

It is often argued that Jesus recognized the inadequacy, the literal untruth, of such titles as "Son of man" and "Messiah" but that he claimed the one and allowed the other to be bestowed on him because they were the only terms available for the communicating of his sense of unique vocation. He had to use these human, historically developed terms, but he did not use them in their accepted sense. They had for him a fresh, highly symbolic meaning, very personal to himself. In particular, he saw the role he was to play as involving vicarious suffering, and was concerned to transform the conception of the Son of man-Messiah by identifying him with the Suffering Servant. This line of argument deserves respect—if for no other reason, because so many distinguished scholars have followed it—but it is far from convincing. Why does not the Gospel evidence make this intention of Jesus more nearly unmistakable? Why do so many of the occurrences of the phrase "Son of man" in the Gospels conform so simply and completely to apocalyptic usage? Why is Jesus represented as saying so little about the Servant? Would it have seemed in the interest of effective communication to use terms which he understood in ways radically different from those in which his hearers understood them? Other such questions could be asked. Besides, one must recognize that if the title "Son of man," however transformed, designated in any sense a super-human person, the psychological difficulties we have been discussing cannot be denied.

V

One must also ask whether there is not something unnatural, not to say morbid, in the kind of thoughts about his death which scholars who take this position often attribute—indeed, almost have to attribute—to Jesus. I am not referring here simply to the conception of it as being in some sense vicarious. The idea of vicarious suffering is not alien to Hebrew-Jewish religion—obviously, the whole cult of animal sacrifice implies it. It is true that human sacrifice had been rejected with horror long before the time of Christ; but the idea that the death of one person might in some way atone for the sins of all, or many, would not have been in first-century Judaism, or probably in the Judaism of any earlier period, an impossible, or even strange, conception.

Sometimes Exod. 32:31-32 is cited in this connection: Moses' prayer to Yahweh, "Alas, this people have sinned a great sin; they have made for themselves gods of gold. But now, if thou wilt forgive their sin—and if not, blot me, I pray thee, out of thy book which thou hast written." But the point here, although not unrelated, is obviously quite a different one. It is not that Moses believes he can possibly atone for the people's sin by his death, but that he wants to suffer with them any punishment Yahweh may decree, the guiltless with the guilty. Neither is II Sam. 24:17, also sometimes referred to in this same connection, really apropos. Here David protests against Yahweh's visiting on the people as a whole a punishment which he alone incurred: "Lo, I have sinned, and I have done wickedly; but these sheep, what have they done? Let thy hand, I pray thee, be against me. . . ." The book of IV Maccabees, however, written near the beginning of the Christian era, contains unmistakable traces of the conception that the suffering of one may avail for all. At one point (6:28) Eleazar, who is being tortured for his faith, cries out in his death throes: "Be merciful unto thy people, and let our punishment be a satisfaction in their behalf. Make my blood their purification, and take my soul

73

to ransom their souls." Later in the same work (17:21-22) it
is said of the martyrs that they "became a ransom for our
nation's sin; and through the blood of these righteous men
and the propitiation of their death, the divine Providence
delivered Israel. . . ." When Paul (in Rom. 9:3) cries out in
"anguish": "I could wish that I myself were accursed and cut
off from Christ for the sake of my brethren, my kinsmen by
race," he shows familiarity with this same idea; and it is very
doubtful that this familiarity grows simply out of his reflection
as a Christian upon the death of Christ. Indeed, would it be
possible to understand the primitive community's ascription
of vicarious sacrificial value to *this* death if the general conception had not already been present in both the Jewish and
the Hellenistic worlds?

It is worth noting perhaps that although Paul shows familiarity with the general idea of one person's suffering for the nation,
he seems to take for granted that it would be impossible for
him actually to be that person. And in IV Maccabees, it is
others than the martyrs themselves who say they "became a
ransom for our nation's sins." To be sure, Eleazar is represented
as speaking for himself in praying that his soul may be taken
"to ransom" the souls of others, but no reader of that homi-
letical work will need to be informed that the coherent and
fairly extensive speech attributed to a man in the final throes
of being burned to death can hardly be historical. In other
words, although there is evidence of the prevalence of the
conception of vicariously atoning death, we do not find anyone's
actually interpreting his own death in that way. Still, the
possibility of one's doing so is certainly implied.

When I say, then, that there is something morbid about the
thoughts concerning his sufferings which we often ascribe to
Jesus, I am not referring to any conception he may have had

74

of the possible vicarious value of his cruel death, especially when, during the last days or hours, the necessity of bearing it inescapably confronted him. What seems morbid and unnatural is the *choice* of such a death, the *purpose* to suffer it, which are commonly attributed to him. Is it easy to believe that from the mid-point of his career onward, if not from the beginning,[22] he moved consciously and deliberately toward his Passion? Such an "intention" almost has to be ascribed to him if he is thought of as identifying himself with the Servant of the Lord. But how could he have known he would be killed? His death, after all, was the consequence of the action and interaction of various historical and political forces; and although it may have been predetermined or even divinely predestined, how could any human being have known that? To be sure, we can readily ascribe to him a recognition of the danger of death, as well as a willingness to incur it if the will of God should lead to it. On that account, we may believe, "he set his face to go to Jerusalem." But the Synoptic Gospel accounts of the final week clearly indicate that he did not refrain from taking precautions against arrest, and the prayer in Gethsemane would seem to show that he was remembered to have hoped even up to the very end that the bitter cup might not need to be drunk. This is the kind of attitude we should have expected of him and, in our right minds, have desired. But it is not an attitude consistent with the view that Jesus thought of himself as the Servant-Messiah—that he knew he

[22] Some writers, concluding that the early Church saw in Jesus' baptism an anticipation and a symbol of his Passion and the moment when he consecrated himself to the role that would lead to the Cross, go so far as to attribute such an understanding of it to Jesus himself. See O. Cullmann, *Baptism in the New Testament* (London: S.C.M. Press, 1950), pp. 9-22; J. A. T. Robinson, "Baptism as a Category of New Testament Soteriology," *Scottish Journal of Theology*, VI (1953), 257 ff.; and O. Cullmann, *Early Christian Worship* (London: S.C.M. Press, 1953), pp. 59-66.

must be put to death in order to fulfill his vocation, that he "interpreted his destiny as that of the suffering redeemer, as the representative of the many whose supreme need is reconciliation to God." [23] Such an understanding of his destiny is compatible with the theology—and the psychology—of the Church. But is it compatible with the mental health of the man Jesus?

VI

Although these difficulties vary in seriousness according to the various ways in which the phrases involved, especially the "Son of man," are understood, and may be regarded as never in themselves decisive, they should be recognized as bearing in an important way upon our evaluation of the Gospel evidence. The fact that there are difficulties of this kind standing in the way of our believing that Jesus thought of himself as the divine Son of man or of his death as the representative death of the Messiah, whereas it would have been expected that the Church eventually would have thought of him in some such way in any case—this fact does not settle the issue, but it creates a presumption which needs to be acknowledged and clearly refuted by those who ascribe the substance of the Church's christological faith to Jesus himself. We turn now to a somewhat fuller examination of the Gospel evidence bearing on this issue than we have thus far had occasion to make.

[23] Taylor, *op. cit.,* p. 282.

CHAPTER FOUR

The Gospel Evidence

ENOUGH HAS ALREADY BEEN SAID TO INDICATE THAT THE IMPOR-
tant questions to be asked of the Gospels, so far as our present
inquiry is concerned, are first, Did Jesus believe himself to be
the Son of man in some unique sense of that term (whether
apocalyptic or some other) ? And, second, Did he regard himself
as also fulfilling the prophetic image of the Suffering Servant
of Isa. 53? The present chapter will be largely devoted to an
examination of the Gospels with these two questions in mind.

I

First, however, we must briefly deal with a third question,
raised and summarily answered at the beginning of the preceding chapter but deserving somewhat fuller examination
than was appropriate then—namely, the question whether
Jesus may not have believed himself to be the Messiah in the
traditional sense of a supernaturally chosen and endowed ruler
of the people. When this question was raised before, I pointed
to the paucity of references to the Messiah among Jesus'
recorded words (as compared with his allusions to the Son
of man). Assuming, as I think we must, that these two terms
represented rather different and basically incompatible ways
of thinking of God's agent in the eschatological fulfillment,
we concluded that if Jesus identified himself with any figure in

contemporary Jewish speculation about the coming of God's kingdom, it was not with the Messiah, as an essentially human figure, a "Son of David," but with the divine Son of man. But there is some Gospel evidence to the contrary, and something needs to be said about this evidence before we turn to the more complicated issues with which this chapter is to be largely concerned. We need to deal here with two sayings and with two incidents in Jesus' career. These four items do not, of course, comprise the whole material of the Gospels in which Jesus' identification of himself with the Son of David-Messiah seems to be implied; but they are certainly the primary and decisive items.

Of the two sayings the first is Jesus' response to the confession of Peter at Caesarea Philippi as Matthew records it (16:17). According to Mark (upon whom both Matthew and Luke are manifestly dependent at this point), Jesus had asked his disciples, "Who do men say that I am?" and they had answered with "John the Baptist," or "Elijah," or "one of the prophets." Jesus had then asked, "But who do you say that I am?" Peter's reply was, "You are the Christ" (8:27-29). Now it is commonly assumed that Jesus accepted this title; but only in Matthew is it stated that he did, and this statement belongs to a paragraph (16:17-24) apparently inserted into the Marcan story and bearing many marks of its later origin. In Mark (whom Luke follows here) we read only that after Peter's confession Jesus "charged [his disciples] to tell no one about him." We are then told that "he began to teach them that the Son of man must suffer many things, and be rejected by the elders and the chief priests . . ."—a passage which could be interpreted as a repudiation of the whole role of the Messiah, in which such suffering had no part. In the same way, Jesus' stern rebuke of Peter, who deprecated this talk of suffering, could be understood as a rejection of the Messiah's role. After all, if Peter is right in calling Jesus Messiah, he would seem to be right in his protests. There is thus a consistency in Mark's story which Matthew's lacks. If Jesus can commend Peter for recognizing him as the Messiah, as he does in Matthew, how can he so sternly reprove him for expecting him to fulfill the office he has accepted? [1]

Of course, Mark unquestionably believed that Jesus was the Messiah (as well as Son of man), and would not have doubted that Jesus himself fully accepted Peter's ascription. The fact, therefore, that this Gospel does not, and probably cannot, actually quote Jesus as doing so is particularly significant. And it is certainly conceivable that Jesus' command of silence about his messiahship has taken the place in Mark of an original denial on Jesus' part of the messiahship itself. Such a denial, of course, could never have become a part of the tradition. It would have been incredible that Jesus had made it.

Whether an actual conversation lies back of the Marcan story of Peter's confession, it is impossible, of course, to be certain. But if it did, we may reasonably suppose that three questions were asked, or at any rate answered, and not two only: "What do men say?" "What do you say?" and "What do I say?" and that Jesus' answer to the third question implied a rejection, not only of the popular estimates of his person, cited in response to the first question, but of the disciples' estimate as well.

The second saying which seems to support the hypothesis that Jesus thought of himself as Messiah is found at Mark 14:62. Jesus is being tried by the high priest and has just

[1] See J. Héring, *La royaume de dieu et sa venue* (Paris: Libraire Felix Alcan, 1937), pp. 122 ff.

been asked, "Are you the Christ, the Son of the Blessed?" He answers, "I am [ἐγώ εἰμι]; and you will see the Son of man sitting at the right hand of Power, and coming with the clouds of heaven." This is the only place in the Synoptic Gospels where Jesus is recorded as clearly and emphatically accepting the title of Messiah. The passage must be given its due weight, but it is scarcely important enough to outweigh the silence of Jesus or the ambiguity of his reply at every other place where the messiahship is an issue. Given the fact that the Gospel writers and the whole Church for which and to which they spoke took for granted that Jesus was the Messiah and knew himself to be such, the striking thing is not that this "I am" appears but that it appears only once.

Some scholars would deny this uniqueness. To be sure, the words "I am" are found only once, but it is argued that the parallels in Matthew and Luke are not less affirmative. Matthew (26:64) records the same answer to the high priest's question as Mark gives except that "You have said so" replaces "I am"; and Luke, in what looks like the parallel passage (22:70), has "You say that I am." Goodspeed translates σὺ εἶπας at Matt. 26:64 as "It is true," and ὑμεῖς λέγετε ὅτι ἐγώ εἰμι at Luke 22:70 as "I am, as you say." These expressions are taken in the same affirmative way by The Twentieth Century New Testament and by Moffatt, and by other modern translations. It is on the surface, however, not easy to believe that σὺ εἶπας or any similar expression could have been as unequivocal as "I am," and study of the question confirms this doubt.[2] There is virtually no evidence that σὺ εἶπας meant "yes" except what are felt to be the implications of these very passages. Goodspeed argues that the Matthaean (and Lucan)

[2] See Morton Smith, "Goodspeed's 'Problems of New Testament Translation,'" *Journal of Biblical Literature,* LXIV, 506-10.

expressions must have been as positive, and as clearly positive, as the Marcan; otherwise the later evangelists would have let Mark's phrase stand unchanged. Certainly they would not have been disposed to weaken Jesus' answer.[3] Morton Smith makes some suggestions as to possible motives of such a weakening: for example, that Matthew may have wanted to show that Jesus was not technically guilty of a treasonable claim. But one might ask whether the more natural way to guard against such misinterpretation of his messiahship would not have been to make clear, as the Fourth Gospel does, that his kingdom was "not of this world." To me it seems more likely that the text of Mark which Matthew and Luke were following read, not ἐγώ εἰμι, but rather σὺ εἶπας ὅτι ἐγώ εἰμι, in accordance with a not unimpressive list of ancient witnesses (Θ Φ *pc* arm Or). Both the Matthaean and the Lucan texts (as well as the alternative Marcan text) could obviously have been very naturally derived from this reading; and it becomes unnecessary either to explain why Matthew and Luke "weakened" Mark's christological statement or to maintain that no weakening was involved—two undertakings almost equally difficult. But however one accounts for the textual phenomena, it remains clear that no decisive weight can be ascribed to the "I am" of Mark 14:62.

I have said that two incidents in the Gospel narrative call for some attention in this same connection. These are Jesus' so-called triumphal entry into Jerusalem (Mark 11:1-11 and parallels) and his cleansing of the Temple (Mark 11:15-19 and parallels). There can be no doubt that, in the view of the Gospel writers, both of these actions of Jesus were conscious acts of the Messiah and indeed were intended—the first entirely

[3] See E. J. Goodspeed, *Problems of New Testament Translation* (University of Chicago Press, 1945), pp. 64-68.

and the second in part—as public declarations of his messiahship. It is by no means clear, however, that the original incidents had this meaning or intention—although some witnesses, even then, may have interpreted them so.

One can see the heightening of the messianic element as we move from Mark to the later Gospels. Into the Marcan story of the triumphal entry, Matthew introduces the messianic prediction from Zechariah 9:9, finding it fulfilled in Jesus' riding on a donkey (ὄνος). Mark had earlier used simply a word for "horse" (πῶλος) and apparently had no thought of the Zechariah prophecy.[4] The passage Mark does quote is a verse or two from Ps. 118, a priestly benediction without any particular messianic significance (although, of course, Mark understood it messianically): "Hosanna! . . . Blessed be he who comes in the name of the Lord!" But Matthew (21:1-11) makes this messianic meaning more explicit by inserting "the Son of David" after "Hosanna"; and Luke, who in this passage as a whole has followed Mark much more closely, sharpens the messianic sense at this point by introducing (according to most manuscripts) the word "king" into the words of the psalm: "Blessed be the King who comes in the name of the Lord!" (19:38). The Fourth Gospel (12:12-16), besides keeping the allusion to Zech. 9:9 which Matthew introduced into Mark, describes the welcoming crowd of disciples as carrying palm branches, a definite messianic or kingly symbol.[5] This Gospel also tells us frankly (12:16) that Jesus' disciples did not understand what was happening at the time. Only later did they recognize the messianic significance of Jesus' way of entering the city.

[4] See Walter Bauer, "The 'Colt' of Palm Sunday," *Journal of Biblical Literature,* LXXII, 220-29.

[5] See W. R. Farmer, "The Palm Branches in John 12:13," *The Journal of Theological Studies,* New Series, III, 62-66.

As for the cleansing of the Temple, the story in Mark contains no suggestion of its being a messianic act (although again it must be recognized that Mark undoubtedly understood it so) ; and Luke again closely follows Mark. In Matthew, however, the messianic meaning is again made explicit. Instead of Mark's: "And the chief priests and the scribes heard it and sought a way to destroy him," we find (in Matt. 21:15-16) :

But when the chief priests and the scribes saw the wonderful things that he did, and the children crying out in the temple, "Hosanna to the Son of David!" they were indignant; and they said to him, "Do you hear what these are saying?" And Jesus said to them, "Yes; have you never read,
       'Out of the mouth of babes and sucklings
       thou hast brought perfect praise.'?"

In the Fourth Gospel the incident is seen as a sign of Jesus' divine authority and of the displacement of Judaism by the new faith: "Destroy this temple, and in three days I will raise it up."

When one can so clearly see, as in these cases, the effects of Christian faith upon the way in which a story is told in the later Gospels, one is bound to recognize the probability that even the earliest form of the story is not free from the same effects. Not infrequently indeed one is justified in suspecting that such a story in its entirety is the creation of faith. Such skepticism is not called for in these cases, however. It is altogether likely that actual incidents lay back of these two Gospel pericopes and that these incidents were not unlike what Mark has described. But this only means that when Jesus entered Jerusalem, he was hailed by a group of Passover pilgrims, presumably Galileans, as "the prophet Jesus from Nazareth of Galilee" (so Matt. 21:11), or even as Messiah;

83

and that when, a few days later, he observed what seemed to him the desecration of the Temple, he made a vigorous and effective protest.

We have good reason to distrust the suggestion in our sources that these were other than the spontaneous actions—of the welcoming crowd in the one case and of Jesus himself in the other—or that the occasions were in any sense contrived by Jesus. But even if we decide that Jesus planned these dramatic incidents, it does not follow that he did so in order to proclaim himself as Messiah. His purpose may have been to proclaim in a conspicuous and dramatic way (somewhat in the manner of the ancient prophets) the nearness of the kingdom of God and the urgency of God's demand for reform. If Jesus made a conspicuous public entrance into Jerusalem, surrounded by a host of disciples and friendly spectators, and if he made a strong and public protest against the desecration of the Temple, these incidents would obviously have lent themselves perfectly to the uses of later Christian apologetic. They would inevitably have been thought of as deliberate messianic actions, and this meaning would have become progressively more manifest as the stories were told and retold. But neither incident needs to be pictured as originally occurring in such a way as to imply the consciousness of messiahship on Jesus' part; and in view of the many indications that he did not characteristically think in messianic terms (that is, "messianic" in the strict sense), we have every reason to ascribe the messianic implications in the narratives to the "tendency" of the Gospel writers.

I have just spoken of the indications that Jesus did not find traditional messianic terms congenial. The most important of these is, of course, the relative paucity of the use of the term "Messiah" in the records of Jesus' teaching despite its prevalence among the Christians at the time when the Gospel tradition was taking form.[6] Everyone acknowledges this paucity and recognizes that it carries a negative significance of some kind. Most scholars have taken the position, referred to briefly near the end of the preceding chapter, that although Jesus knew he was the Messiah, he conceived of messiahship in a radically new way. For this reason, he was in a double mind about the term itself: on the one hand, he tended to avoid it and never used it of himself; but on the other, he could not bring himself to reject it when others applied it to him. But such a view attributes to Jesus an indecisiveness which I should say is neither characteristic of him nor understandable in his situation. If he thought of himself as the Messiah, but in a new sense, would he not, instead of avoiding the term, have devoted a good deal of effort to explaining the new sense? And would not the necessity of such explanation have led to more frequent appearances of the term in his teaching than if the common meaning had been assumed. Actually, there is no evidence whatever that Jesus tried to invest the term "Messiah" with a new significance—to explain what kind of "king" he was (the brief explanation in John 18:33-37 serves only to call attention to the complete absence of anything like it in the earlier Gospels). We must conclude that Jesus did not think in terms of a personal Messiah, a David or Moses or Elijah redivivus. If his expectation of the coming judgment and salvation included a personal mediator or agent of God's action, that mediator or agent was not the traditional human Messiah, but the divine Son of man.

And so we return to the questions about the Son of man and the Suffering Servant which were asked at the beginning of this chapter.

[6] See above, p. 57.

II

The many occurrences of the phrase "Son of man" in the Gospels together form a complicated and perplexing picture— or better, perhaps a kind of jigsaw picture puzzle to which no one has proposed a really satisfactory solution. The solution is elusive partly because some of the pieces are missing; but more perhaps because other pieces had their original shapes altered, even before the Gospels took form, so that they might better fit what was then and has continued to be the orthodox solution. Since these pieces do not quite fit, the orthodox solution falls short of satisfying; but since the pieces have been altered, the original picture is probably lost forever. Certainly it cannot be recovered with complete clarity or assurance.

We have seen that the phrase "Son of man" is found some seventy times in the Synoptic Gospels, and invariably on Jesus' lips. No other character in the narratives refers to the Son of man, nor do the several Gospel writers themselves, or for that matter the writers of the epistles. This striking fact creates a very strong presumption that Jesus was actually remembered to have used the phrase and that he used it with some seriousness and impressiveness. The early Church can hardly be thought of as originating the phrase and then confining it so narrowly to Jesus' own usage.

Now, of the numerous occurrences of the phrase in Jesus' teaching it is obvious that for our present purpose of trying to get at the original facts, we should disregard mere repetitions of Mark in Matthew and in Luke and that we should reduce by one our total count wherever Matthew and Luke are apparently following a second common source. In other words, the significant occurrences are those in Mark, in what is called

Q, and in the materials peculiar to Matthew and Luke. These occurrences add up to forty-one, and it is with them that we are really concerned.

These forty-one occurrences divide themselves at once into three classes. Twenty times the Son of man is referred to in what is clearly the general context of apocalypticism: his exaltation at God's right hand is being affirmed, or his coming on the clouds of heaven is being predicted. There are three of these cases in Mark (8:38; 13:26; 14:62),[7] four in Q (Luke 11:30; 12:40; 17:24, 26), eight (with some doubt in one case) in Matthew alone (10:23; 13:41; 16:28; 19:28; 24:30 [twice], 39; 25:31), and five in Luke alone (12:8; 17:22, 30; 18:8; 21:36). These passages together belong to a quite distinct and easily recognizable category and can be readily isolated. We shall call this group "A."

Among the rest of the passages, another group of sayings now emerges almost equally clearly. These are also for the most part predictions, but they have to do with the suffering which Jesus (in these cases the reference to him is unmistakable) is to undergo, his approaching trial and execution: "the Son of man must suffer." These passages are virtually confined to Mark (8:31; 9:12, 31; 10:33, 45; 14:21, 41) and parallels. The conception of the suffering Son of man is not found at all in Q and occurs outside the Marcan material only at Matt. 26:2, Luke 17:25 and 24:7—each time in what is almost certainly an editorial construction. In other words, whereas the allusions to the glorified Son of man are found in all the strata

[7] Mark 9:9 is often included here, but it seems to me to belong in another category and will be found there. It probably does not need to be said that, except at a few points, no originality can be claimed for my way of either analyzing or interpreting the appearances of "Son of man" in the Synoptic Gospels. I am indebted to more scholars than I could name: Lietzmann, Bultmann, Grant, and many more—the most recent of them R. H. Fuller.

of the Synoptic Gospel tradition, the references to the suffering Son of man (we shall call them the "B" group) seem originally to have belonged only to Mark. It is also very important to note that the two sets of passages, supporting respectively the two conceptions of the Son of man, are readily separable and quite distinct from each other. Those passages which speak of the Coming One do not refer to his suffering, and those which are concerned with the suffering of the Son of man make no mention of his exaltation or of his glorious coming. The single exception here, Luke 17:25, is one of the most clearly editorial passages in the entire Synoptic Gospel tradition. Thus, the terms "A" and "B" stand, not merely for two very distinctive ways of conceiving of the Son of man, but also for two quite distinct groups of actual sayings.

The third group ("C") is made up of eleven miscellaneous sayings not belonging to either "A" or "B."

The following exhibit, which includes the actual text of the passages referred to, will perhaps make the results of this analysis more easily available:

THE SON OF MAN SAYINGS IN THE SYNOPTIC GOSPELS

A. *The Apocalyptic Son of Man*

MARK   Mark 8:38: ". . . of him will the Son of man also be ashamed, when he comes in the glory of his Father with the holy angels."

Mark 13:26: "And then they will see the Son of man coming in clouds with great power and glory."

Mark 14:62: "You will see the Son of man sitting at the right hand of Power, and coming with the clouds of heaven."

Q	Luke 11:30:	"As Jonah became a sign . . . , so will the Son of man be to this generation."
	Luke 12:40:	"The Son of man is coming at an hour you do not expect."
	Luke 17:24:	"As the lightning flashes and lights up the sky from one side to the other, so will the Son of man be in his day."
	Luke 17:26:	"As it was in the days of Noah, so will it be in the days of the Son of man."
MATT. ALONE	Matt. 10:23:	". . . you will not have gone through all the towns of Israel, before the Son of man comes."
	Matt. 13:41:	"The Son of man will send his angels . . . ."
	Matt. 16:28:	"There are some standing here who will not taste death before they see the Son of man coming in his kingdom."
	Matt. 19:28:	"Truly, . . . in the new world, when the Son of man shall sit on his glorious throne . . . ."
	Matt. 24:29-30:	". . . the powers of the heavens will be shaken; then will appear the sign of the Son of man in heaven . . . ."
	Matt. 24:30:	". . . they will see the Son of man coming on the clouds of heaven with power and great glory."
	Matt. 24: 39:	". . . so will be the coming of the Son of man."
	Matt. 25:31:	"When the Son of man comes in his glory. . . ."
LUKE ALONE	Luke 12:8:	". . . everyone who acknowledges me before men, the Son of man will also acknowledge before the angels of God."

	Luke 17:22:	"The days are coming when you will desire to see one of the days of the Son of man . . . ."
	Luke 17:30:	". . . so will it be on the day when the Son of man is revealed."
	Luke 18:8:	". . . when the Son of man comes, will he find faith on earth?"
	Luke 21:36:	". . . praying that you may have strength to escape all these things . . . and to stand before the Son of man."

B. *The Suffering Son of Man*

MARK	Mark 8:31:	". . . the Son of man must suffer . . . ."
	Mark 9:12:	". . . how is it written of the Son of man, that he should suffer many things . . . ."
	Mark 9:31:	"The Son of man will be delivered into the hands of men, and they will kill him . . . ."
	Mark 10:33:	"The Son of man will be delivered to the chief priests and the scribes, and they will condemn him to death."
	Mark 10:45:	"The Son of man . . . came . . . to serve, and to give his life as a ransom for many."
	Mark 14:21:	"The Son of man goes as it is written of him, but woe to that man by whom the Son of man is betrayed!"
	Mark 14:41:	". . . the Son of man is betrayed into the hands of sinners."
ELSE-WHERE	Matt. 26:2:	"You know that after two days the Passover is coming, and the Son of man will be delivered up to be crucified."

Luke 17:25:   "But first he must suffer many things and be rejected by this generation."

Luke 24:6-7:   "Remember how he told you, while he was still in Galilee, that the Son of man must be delivered into the hands of sinful men, and be crucified . . . ."

C. *The Remaining Son of Man Sayings*

MARK

Mark 2:10:   ". . . that you may know that the Son of man has authority on earth to forgive sins . . . ."

Mark 2:27-28:   "The sabbath was made for man, not man for the sabbath; so the Son of man is lord even of the sabbath."

Mark 9:9:   "As they were coming down the mountain, he charged them to tell no one what they had seen, until the Son of man should have risen from the dead."

Q

Luke 7:34:   "The Son of man has come eating and drinking . . . ."

Luke 9:58:   "Foxes have holes, and birds of the air have nests; but the Son of man has nowhere to lay his head."

Luke 12:10:   "And every one who speaks a word against the Son of man will be forgiven; but he who blasphemes against the Holy Spirit will not be forgiven."

ELSE-
WHERE

Matt. 13:37:   "He who sows the good seed is the Son of man" (explanation of the parable of the tares).

Matt. 16: 13:   ". . . Jesus . . . asked his disciples, 'Who do men say that the Son of man is?' "

Luke 6:22:	"Blessed are you when men hate you . . . on account of the Son of man."
Luke 19:10:	"For the Son of man came to seek and to save the lost."
Luke 22:48:	"Judas, would you betray the Son of man with a kiss?"

III

It will be useful to look at each of these three groups of sayings separately before attempting any generalizations about Jesus' meaning as a whole. The sayings in group "A" would appear to be the most clearly authentic (except possibly for several of the scattered sayings in "C") and, if authentic, the most significant. Both of these points have been disputed, but each seems to me to be easily defensible. As regards authenticity, one may point out that here are no fewer than twenty sayings (not counting parallels), many more than in either of the other two groups—indeed, almost as many as in both groups together—which clearly belong in the context of apocalyptic expectation (whether we think Daniel or Enoch more important does not greatly matter at this point). They refer unmistakably to the exalted status of the Son of man or to his expected coming on the clouds of heaven. If there were any evidence that the primitive churches, or even any significant number of them, were made up of persons who had earlier embraced a Son of man apocalypticism and who would therefore be quick to interpret their Christian experience and hopes in terms of it, we might with some confidence account for these sayings in that way. But there is no evidence of this kind; indeed, the striking silence about the Son of man on the part of everyone in the New Testament except Jesus himself looks definitely the other way. It is hard to avoid the conclusion that Jesus was remembered to have expected and to have predicted the coming of the glorious Son of man. That figure apparently belonged to his way of visualizing the imminent coming of the kingdom of God. If this is not true and all the evidence clearly supporting this conclusion must be dismissed as "secondary," then there ceases to be any reason for believing that Jesus used the phrase "Son of man" as a title at all—whether for himself or for another.

But if he used it in speaking of God's agent in the imminent judgment and redemption, it would seem equally undeniable that the passages in which he does so, the "A" group of sayings, are also the most significant so far as the Gospel usage as a whole is concerned. It is clear that the title, wherever used, carries an exalted and a solemn meaning. As we shall see a little later, there can be no doubt that an original "I" in Jesus' remembered teaching was often changed to the "Son of man" and thus made more solemnly impressive. Unless the sayings in group "A" are relied on to account for this significance of the title, the Gospels leave us without any hint of an explanation. It is, of course, conceivable that Jesus actually used the phrase as a title only in a highly sophisticated Ezekielic sense (so Duncan) or in an equally esoteric and enigmatic corporate sense (so T. W. Manson), and that its use in the context of apocalypticism was a later development to give his usage a more definite and familiar meaning; but such conceptions imply the original inauthenticity of these passages as they stand. If Jesus actually expected and spoke of the coming of the Son of man, one can hardly doubt that it was this meaning which gives weight and tone to the title in other connections, whether in Jesus' own usage or in the tradition of his teaching.[8]

[8] It is sometimes argued that the writers of our Gospels, being probably Greeks, were not conversant with Enoch or with apocalyptic ideas and images

Two additional remarks need to be made about this group of sayings. The first is that nowhere among them does Jesus identify himself, whether explicitly or by implication, with the Son of man. Not only is that personage always spoken of in the third person, but some of the passages hardly permit of any other possibility.[9] We have seen that the Gospel writers apparently sometimes substitute the "Son of man" for an original "I," but there is absolutely no evidence that this has been done in the case of any of the "A" passages. Jesus is nowhere reported as saying, "*I* shall come on the clouds of heaven," or, "*I* shall be exalted at the right hand of God's throne." There are a few passages that point to a close and mysterious connection between Jesus and the Son of man; but even these, not only do not identify the two, but may be thought of as actually accentuating the distinction.[10]

---

of the kind which Enoch (esp. chs. 37–71) represents. They would not have recognized "the Son of man" as an apocalyptic title, and therefore what I have just been saying about the normativeness of the use of the phrase in the "A" passages would not have been true for them. For these Gospel writers and their communities "the Son of man" on Jesus' lips would have seemed as enigmatic as the Greek phrase sounded strange upon their own. The Aramaic term was literally translated without any understanding of its meaning; it was simply, for whatever reason, Jesus' mysterious way of speaking of himself. All of this may be true; on the other hand, it may involve an exaggeration of the distance separating the Gospel writers from the original Palestinian environment of Christianity. But whatever our conclusions here, will it not be agreed that at earlier stages in the development of the tradition the apocalyptic connotations of the phrase were certainly recognized and that the original prestige of the title as applied to Jesus must be so explained? It is possible, however, that the key to understanding why only Jesus uses the title in the written Gospels is the fact that it had no meaning for the Gospel writers except as Jesus' own chosen way of referring to himself in his august role.

[9] Matt. 13:41 when taken with 13:37 would seem to be an exception here. But this passage, the allegorical interpretation of the parable of the tares, is almost certainly "secondary" and is usually so described.

[10] I have in mind especially Mark 8:38 (equals Luke 9:26): "For whoever is ashamed of me and of my words, in this adulterous and sinful generation, of him will the Son of man also be ashamed, when he comes in the glory of the Father

The second remark is that there can be no doubt whatever that the Gospel writers, and probably their major sources, took entirely for granted that Jesus was referring to himself in these passages—that he was, and knew himself to be, the apocalyptic Son of man. It was inevitable, therefore, that they should identify the Son of man in this way, regardless of whether Jesus did so or not. He was remembered to have spoken of the coming of the Son of man, and nothing could have seemed more certain to the first believers than that this so far unfulfilled prediction would be fulfilled. But who will this Son of man be? The answer would have seemed so obvious that the question would hardly have been asked. At the time when Jesus had spoken of the coming of the Son of man, his hearers may have supposed that he was speaking of another; but now it would be clear that he had been speaking of himself. He was speaking of his own return after his death from the exalted place at God's right hand to which he was to be raised.

My own conclusion from all of these reflections is that if we had only the "A" class of Son of man sayings, we should surmise first that Jesus expected and spoke of the coming of the Son of man, a heavenly being who would be God's agent in the imminent eschatological event; second, that he did not identify himself with this personage; but third, that the first Christians did make this identification immediately after the Resurrection and, naturally and inevitably, ascribed it also to him.

---

with the holy angels"; and Luke 12:8-9: "Everyone who acknowledges me before men, the Son of man also will acknowledge before the angels of God; but he who denies me before men will be denied before the angels of God." If these sayings go back to Jesus himself in just their present form, they undoubtedly point to his consciousness of what Héring (*op. cit.*, p. 96) calls "a soteriological connection between his earthly mission and the coming of the Son of Man," but they clearly stop short of making an identification. But note Matt. 10:32, where, in a not dissimilar saying, the first personal pronoun is used throughout.

IV

Because of the special importance for this particular study of the sayings in the "B" class, sayings about the suffering of the Son of man, and for other reasons, it will be best to leave them till the last, and to consider next the miscellaneous sayings in the "C" group. There are three of these in Mark (2:10; 2:27-28; 9:9), three in Q (Luke 7:34; 9:58; 12:10), and five peculiar to either Matthew or Luke (Matt. 13:37; 16:13; Luke 6:22; 19:10; 22:48). In all of these sayings Jesus refers to the Son of man without explicit reference to either the Passion or the Parousia. I have called them miscellaneous, and so they are as compared with those in the other categories, but a few generalizations are possible. One notices that, like the apocalyptic Son of man sayings, these instances are drawn from every strata of the Gospel tradition, although one cannot be sure exactly how far the sayings peculiar to Matthew and Luke belong to earlier sources or represent editorial work on the part of the authors of these Gospels. One observes also that whereas the sayings in the other two categories do not begin to appear in Mark before 8:31, and appear only a little earlier in Matthew and Luke, these more neutral, or miscellaneous, sayings are found both early and late. It may also be said of these sayings, not only that the Gospel writers understand Jesus to be referring to himself as the Son of man, but also that, *if the sayings are genuine as they stand,* Jesus was in fact speaking of himself.

There are grave reasons for suspicion, however, that the sayings are not genuine as they stand. In at least three of the cases (Matt. 16:13; Luke 6:22; 7:34), the phrase "Son of man" seems to stand simply for "I," and one must suspect that in such cases it has been substituted for an original personal pronoun.[11] Indeed, one can virtually see the substitution taking place in Luke 6:22 and Matt. 16:13. In other cases (for example, Mark 9:9; Matt. 13:37; Luke 19:10; 22:48[?]) the phrase almost certainly falls within an editorial addition. One cannot accept as true the several points made in our discussion of the "A" sayings without recognizing that there would have been a strong tendency in the tradition toward editorial change of this kind. Jesus was remembered to have referred to the coming of the Son of man and was now understood to be referring to himself when he did so. It was only to be expected that he would have used the same solemn phrase in referring to himself in other connections. So much can be said about seven of these miscellaneous occurrences of the "Son of man."

This leaves four cases, all of them in Mark or Q. Now it is a well-known fact that the phrase "son of man," while it was used in certain circles as a title of an individual, could mean simply "man," both in a generic or qualitative sense and in the sense of "a man." [12] And it is a striking fact that in all four of these cases, one is given some ground for suspecting an original use of the phrase in this general or ordinary sense. The clearest instance of this perhaps is found in Mark 2:28:

[11] One might also account for Luke 22:48 in this way, although it is just as plausible perhaps to regard this reference to the Son of man as an editorial echo of Mark 14:21. In that case, the saying might more appropriately be placed under B. One must note also here the possibility that in Aramaic "son of man" could be used as a periphrasis for "I." I have no competence here and must depend upon such authorities as Lietzmann and Héring. But note that Sjöberg gravely doubts the possibility of this usage (*op. cit.,* p. 239).

[12] See A. Meyer, *Jesu Muttersprache* (Freiburg and Leipzig, 1896), pp. 91-101; N. Schmidt, "Was *barnasha* a Messianic Title?" *Journal of Biblical Literature,* XV (1896), 36-53; H. Lietzmann, *Der Menschensohn* (Freiburg and Leipzig, 1896), pp. 81-95; J. Wellhausen, *Das Evangelium Marci* (Berlin: Von Georg Reimer, 1903), pp. 17-18, 22; Joseph Klausner, *Jesus of Nazareth* (New York: The Macmillan Co., 1925), pp. 256-57.

"And he said to them, 'The sabbath was made for man, not man for the sabbath; so the Son of man is lord even of the sabbath.' " Needless to say, as the text stands, "the Son of man" refers to Jesus himself; but the context clearly gives some reason for wondering whether in the original form of the utterance it did not appear as a synonym for "man." If that was true, once the phrase came to be understood in the more individual and solemn sense, the whole form of the saying would naturally be altered to accommodate this new meaning.[13] The same possibility is likely to occur to one who considers the other instance to the use of "Son of man" in the early part of Mark—this time at 2:10. Four friends of an ill man have just lowered him into Jesus' presence through the broken roof of a house.

And when Jesus saw their faith, he said to the paralytic, "My son, your sins are forgiven." Now some of the scribes were sitting there, questioning in their hearts, "Why does this man speak thus? It is blasphemy! Who can forgive sins but God alone?" And immediately Jesus, perceiving in his spirit that they thus questioned within themselves, said to them, "Why do you question thus in your hearts? Which is easier, to say to the paralytic, 'Your sins are forgiven,' or to say, 'Rise, take up your pallet and walk'? But that you may know that the Son of man has authority on earth to forgive sins"—he said to the paralytic—"I say to you, rise, take up your pallet and go home."

[13] It is important to note the ὥστε ("so" or "so that") at the beginning of the final clause of the saying. Can the use of his particle be understood unless "son of man" means "man"? If it does not, the final clause does not follow logically from the first. An alternative possibility would be to consider that the quotation from Jesus is thought of as ending with 2:28*a*, and that the ὥστε introduces the conclusion *of the evangelist* from the entire pericope, Mark 2:23 ff. But in that case, we should have here an exception to the rule that the evangelists do not themselves speak of the Son of man, and this seems unlikely.

This is a very difficult pericope, and I would not venture any suggestion whatever as to what its original form may have been—much less as to what, if any, actual incident lies back of it. It is striking, however, that the criticism of Jesus' conduct by the scribes turns on what is appropriate or possible *for a man* (note also Matt. 9:8), and that if, in the original form of the pericope, Jesus was being represented as really answering their point, "Son of man" in whatever answer he gave them must have carried something of that same common meaning.

The first of the Q sayings is found at Luke 9:58 (equals Matt. 8:20). Jesus says to a would-be disciple: "Foxes have holes, and birds of the air have nests; but the Son of man has nowhere to lay his head." Just as at Mark 2:28 a contrast seems to be implied between the sabbath and man, and at Mark 2:10 between God and man, so here we may be dealing with what was originally a contrast between the animals and man. The fact that Jesus both in Mark 2:10 and here would be speaking of himself, a particular man, in no way invalidates this suggestion.[14] We do not need to understand him to be speaking of *any* man or of *every* man, but of *this* man, that is, of himself. The second of the Q sayings is at Luke 12:10 (equals Matt. 12:32): "And whoever says a word against the Son of man will be forgiven; but whoever speaks against the Holy Spirit will not be forgiven." This passage would certainly be more intelligible if originally the contrast had been, not between Son of man and the Holy Spirit, but between *man* and the Holy Spirit.[15]

[14] This case may, of course, be explained as another instance of the substitution of "the Son of man" for an original "I," and many readers may prefer that explanation as more simple and plausible.
[15] This possibility is strengthened, I think, when we compare the almost parallel Marcan passage (3:28): "Truly, I say to you, all sins will be forgiven the sons of men, and whatever blasphemies they utter; but whoever blasphemes against the Holy Spirit never has forgiveness." Note "sons of men" in this passage.

The proposal of this common meaning as belonging to the original form of any one of these four sayings would be far less plausible if it stood alone. It is the fact that no fewer than four of the eleven passages in the 'C" class, and these all in Mark and Q, give some reason for our suspecting this meaning—it is this fact which, for me at least, virtually proves the point. The kind of usage which was discussed under "A" determined the normative meaning for the Gospel writers of the phrase "Son of man." There was a tendency, therefore, to interpret the phrase as having that meaning wherever it occurred in the tradition of Jesus' words and indeed to attribute its use to Jesus in solemn references to himself even when the original tradition did not contain it at all. Surely, once the authenticity and the significance of the "A" sayings are acknowledged, this becomes the most plausible way of explaining the phenomena presented by the "C" cases.[16]

V

We are left now only with the sayings in the "B" group— the sayings concerned with the suffering of the Son of man.

[16] One may ask whether it is likely that Jesus would have used the phrase "son of man" to mean "man" or "a man" in view of the fact that he had available, and often used, other ways of referring to "man" and "a man," whereas he is known to have regularly employed this phrase in speaking of the Coming One. In other words, would he have used the same term in such radically different ways? The question is a good one. Furthermore, in connection with it, I recall Dalman's opinion that although *barnasha* might be used to mean "a man," it would not have been the usual term and would have had an archaic sound in first-century Jewish ears. (See G. Dalman, *The Words of Jesus* [Edinburgh: T. and T. Clark, 1909], pp. 234 ff.) But not all Aramaic scholars agree with Dalman here, and we all know how characteristic it is of languages that the same words or phrases have radically different meanings in various contexts. Still, I think we should recognize at least the possibility that Jesus always used another term (than "son of man") when speaking of "man" or "a man" and that this sometimes became "son of man" in the tradition. If this kind of thing can be shown to have happened to Jesus' "I," it might even more readily happen to his "man."

And here the situation is relatively simple because these sayings are confined to Mark (that is, they are not in Q, nor is there any reason to hold that any of them were found in the special sources of Matthew and Luke). Now one of the principal purposes of this Gospel, it is commonly agreed, was to make clear the messianic significance of Jesus' whole career, from the baptism on, as over against an earlier belief that Jesus really became the Messiah only with or after the Resurrection. Of particular interest to the writer was the theological significance of the death of Jesus. This preoccupation with the death and its meaning was of course not confined to Mark, and it can be traced much earlier. But Mark wants to set forth clearly and vividly the fact, not only that Jesus' death was the death of the Messiah, but also that it overshadowed the earthly career. As we have seen, there are those who urge that for Mark and others Jesus' baptism was an anticipation of his death.[17] Certainly after Peter's confession at Caesarea Philippi in 8:27 ff. the Gospel is dominated by the prospect of the Crucifixion. There are three solemn predictions of the Passion in this section of Mark's narrative and many other more incidental references to it. Jesus "had been no victim of the blind hatred and jealousy of the Jerusalem authorities; instead he had marched as a victor to the fray, conscious of his strength and certain of his eventual triumph." [18] It can be argued, of course, that Mark is only reporting the facts about Jesus' own attitude toward his approaching death; but even so, it must be granted that he has a special interest in doing so, and that he is concerned to bring out in the clearest possible way the positive place of the death in the messianic work of Jesus.

[17] See J. A. T. Robinson, "The One Baptism as a Category of New Testament Soteriology," *Scottish Journal of Theology*, VI (1953), 257-74, and footnote 22 in ch. 3, above.

[18] F. C. Grant, *The Earliest Gospel* (Nashville: Abingdon Press, 1943), p. 157.

Now if all of this is true, it is not strange that the death should appear in Mark as the death of the Son of man. That phrase, as understood and used in the Gospel, was Jesus' own solemn way of designating himself as the Messiah. The death, Mark is saying, no less than the Resurrection and exaltation, belonged to the essential destiny of the Son of man. I find myself agreeing with Bultmann and many others that the conception of Jesus as the suffering Son of man (confined as it is to the Marcan material) probably represents a Marcan contribution to the tradition.

Let it be remembered that we are speaking here of a very particular conception, the death of *the Son of man*. My own conclusion that it does not go back to Jesus' own mind must not be understood to imply that Jesus may not have spoken to his disciples of his death or that he did not find the profoundest kind of meaning in it. Something more along this more positive line will be said in the next chapter.

VI

At this point—after dealing with the suffering Son of man in Mark and before taking up the Gospel evidence that Jesus may have thought of himself as the Suffering Servant of Isa. 53—it may be well to consider briefly a question raised, but not discussed, near the beginning of this book: [19] the question whether the association of suffering with the role of the Messiah or Son of man may not belong to pre-Christian times. This possibility, while still rejected by the majority of scholars, does not lack vigorous and distinguished defenders.[20]

[19] See above, p. 35.
[20] Among these may be mentioned W. D. Davies, *Paul and Rabbinic Judaism* (London: S.P.C.K., 1948), pp. 276-84; J. Jeremias, "Zum Problem der Deutung von Jes. 53 im Palästinischen Spätjudentum," in *Aux sources de la tradition chrétienne*, ed. J.-J. von Allmen (Neuchatel: Delachoux & Niestlé, 1950),

Some importance attaches to how the issue is stated. To the question, usually asked, whether the Servant of Isa. 53 was understood among any significant number of pre-Christian Jews as a messianic figure, biblical students, certainly on the whole, have said No,[21] although so eminent a Semitics scholar as Joachim Jeremias can argue vigorously to the contrary.[22] But the issue is not always stated in just this form. Attention is rather focused on the Son of man and upon the question whether that figure is not as such the figure of a sufferer. It is pointed out that in Daniel the exaltation of the Son of man is really a vindication of him after his *sufferings* (that is, the trials of Israel are presupposed), and also that in the Son of man passages in Enoch clear literary reminiscences of the Servant songs of Isaiah are to be found. As regards these reminiscences, however, many who cite them would agree with C. R. North that while "it seems clear that the author of the 'Parables' identified the Servant with the Messianic Son of Man. . . . it is doubtful whether he fully realized the implications of the identification, since there is nowhere any hint that the Son of Man is to suffer." [23] And as for the Danielic figure, such

---

pp. 113-19; Dodd, *op. cit.*, pp. 117, 119; C. F. D. Moule, "From Defendant to Judge—and Deliverer . . . ," *Bulletin of Studiorum Novi Testamenti Societas* III (1952), 40-53; R. H. Fuller, *The Mission and Achievement of Jesus* (London: S.C.M. Press, 1954), pp. 103-8.

[21] The literature here would be enormous. See brief summary statements in C. R. North, *The Suffering Servant in Deutero-Isaiah* (London: Oxford University Press, 1948), pp. 6-9, and Davies, *op. cit.*, pp. 274-75.

[22] *Op. cit.*, pp. 113-19.

[23] *Op. cit.*, p. 8. For a forceful answer to the arguments, especially of Jeremias, that suffering was associated with the conception of the Enochian Son of man, see Sjöberg, *Menschensohn im Äthiopischen Henochbuch* (Lund: C. W. K. Gleerup, 1946), pp. 116-39. R. H. Fuller (*op. cit.*, p. 103) writes: "Jesus suffers not as the one who is already Son of Man but as the one destined to be the Son of Man, as the Son of Man designate." Although Daniel may be held to give some support here (but not for *redemptive* suffering), Enoch does not, for no more is said there about suffering which the Son of man has already undergone than about any still to come.

scholars as Moule and Dodd acknowledge that although suffering is presupposed of the Son of man in that apocalypse, it is suffering despite which *he* is vindicated rather than suffering because of which *others* are redeemed. In other words, there is no evidence of the influence *in any really significant sense* of Isa. 53, and one is left to conclude that even if some "conflation" of the two images of Servant and Son of man had taken place before Christ, the really creative synthesis first occurred either in Jesus' own mind or in that of the primitive Church.

VII

We come, then, to the consideration of the actual evidence in the Gospels that Jesus thought of himself as the Suffering Servant of Second Isaiah. This needs to engage us only briefly, for the evidence is surprisingly meager. I say "surprisingly," because in view of the widespread use in the Church at the end of the first century of the image of the Servant as a means of understanding the Passion and of communicating its meaning, one might have expected that its use would have been liberally attributed to Jesus himself, whether he was actually remembered to have used it or not. There is no need to document the fact that at the time when Matthew, Luke-Acts, I Peter, Hebrews, John, and I Clement were written, Jesus was being thought of as the Servant and his suffering as a sacrifice for the "many" to whom Isaiah refers. We have seen that some modern scholars gravely doubt that this way of understanding Jesus and his death can be traced any earlier.[24]

[24] Reference has been made to C. T. Craig (above, pp. 46-47). See also F. J. Foakes-Jackson and Kirsopp Lake, eds., *The Beginnings of Christianity* (New York: The Macmillan Co., 1920-33), I, 383 ff. For an excellent statement of the case for the early date of this conception see W. Zimmerli and J. Jeremias, *The Servant of the Lord* (London: S.C.M. Press, 1957), esp. pp. 79-104.

The Gospel Evidence

As I have already indicated, I find myself less skeptical and am ready to acknowledge the influence of Isa. 53 on Paul and Mark (although this cannot be proved), and indeed to believe that Jesus had been identified with the Servant in the most primitive preaching. But there is hardly any explicit evidence for this conclusion, and my principal reason for accepting it is a priori: that is, I find it hard to believe that a passage so appropriate as Isa. 53, both for confessional and apologetic purposes, would not have been "found" at once by the first believers, especially as one of their most acute problems was that of understanding and explaining the death of Christ.[25]

But this very consideration—that is, this very recognition of the naturalness and the inevitability of the early Church's use of Isa. 53 *after the event*—places a large burden of proof on any claim that Jesus himself made this same use of the passage; and this burden the meager Gospel evidence is simply not able to bear. Nowhere in Q or in any special source of Matthew or Luke is the Suffering Servant referred to, even by implication. And unless the very idea that "the Son of man must suffer" is held to imply the Servant (as it may do), the only certain, or almost certain, allusion even in Mark to that figure is in 9:12*b*, which obviously interrupts the context and is regarded by many as a gloss.[26] But whether a gloss or not,

[25] The a priori probability of this use of Isa. 53 by the most primitive church would be greatly increased if it should be established that the Qumran sect identified the "Teacher of Righteousness" with the Suffering Servant. This conclusion is argued for by W. H. Brownlee, "Messianic Motifs of Qumran and the New Testament," *New Testament Studies* III (1956), 12 ff., and by others. But see also Millar Burrows, *The Dead Sea Scrolls* (New York: Viking Press, 1955), pp. 266 ff. Burrows allows the possibility but is on the whole skeptical.

[26] The whole verse reads: "Elijah does come first to restore all things; and how is it written of the Son of man, that he should suffer many things and be treated with contempt?" The passage goes on (vs. 13): "But I tell you that Elijah has come . . . ." As I have said above (p. 47), I am ready to acknowledge the

it so clearly reflects Mark's own understanding of the Passion that we can hardly rest much weight upon it as evidence for Jesus' own thought about himself and his death.[27]

Surely if he had seen himself as the Servant, we might expect the signs of his having done so to be clearer and much more numerous. The misgivings growing out of popular understandings of the meaning of the term which are usually cited to explain his reticence about his messiahship would not have stood in the way of the clearest possible claim to be the Servant. And a natural modesty, or the humility of his character, cannot be resorted to as an explanation of his silence because those who ascribe the claim to him have already attributed to him the even bolder claim to be the heavenly Son of man himself.

VIII

The conclusion, then, to which the argument of this chapter has been moving almost from the start and at which it has now arrived is that Jesus did not regard himself as the Servant-Messiah. The Gospel evidence that he did so is too slight to take care of the large burden of proof the affirmative case must carry.

---

probability that Mark 10:45 involves a memory of Isa. 53. The reminiscence of Isa. 42:1 in Mark 1:11 is quite irrelevant. As Craig (*op. cit.*, p. 242) says: "Because we know that there is a connection between Isaiah 42 and 53, we cannot take it for granted that first-century Christians knew it."

[27] Although I know that he would take exception to much in this chapter, I understand C. F. D. Moule to be denying the adequacy of the evidence to establish any conscious connection of Jesus with the Servant when he writes: "Jesus only occasionally spoke of his redemptive work; when he did, it is questionable whether he drew on the words of Isa. 53. But his work *was* redemptive. It was his work and person rather than his words or his quotations which brought this home" ("From Defendant to Judge—and Deliverer. . .," *Bulletin of Studiorum Novi Testamenti Societas*, III (1952), p. 53). This seems to me to be very close to saying that it was within the experience of the primitive Church, which had alone witnessed this work and alone could bear witness to it, that the realization of the aptness of the Servant image first occurred.

We cannot leave the matter there, however. We still have the question: How then *did* Jesus think of himself and, more particularly, of his death? Once we reject the traditional answer, this becomes an enormously difficult question; and anyone who presumes to answer it at all must recognize how precarious his answer must be. Indeed, if the question calls for an answer in terms comparable in definiteness to "Messiah," "Son of man," and "Servant," one can only say that we are ignorant, not only of what those terms were, but also of what they might have been. But the question does not need to be asked in that form. And when we are set free from the assumption that if Jesus had any peculiarly deep sense of vocation, or indeed any deep sense of peculiar vocation, it must have expressed itself in terms of some traditional messianic category —once we are set free from this assumption, we are in position to recognize that there *was* something extraordinary and unique in the consciousness of Jesus, and that later christological development simply cannot be historically understood unless that "something" is taken into account. To a consideration of this extraordinary and unique element we now turn.

CHAPTER FIVE

The Vocation of Jesus

THE PROBLEM OF THIS CHAPTER, ALTHOUGH IT COULD HARDLY be more difficult, can be fairly simply formulated. It is this: How can we conceive of the intention of Jesus or, more generally, his own thoughts about himself and his mission in such a way as to account for the thoughts of others about him, but without ascribing to him the belief that he was either the King-Messiah of Jewish hopes or yet the Son of man? Or to state the question in another way: How can we describe the self-consciousness of Jesus in such fashion as to make natural and understandable the beliefs of the early Church about him without ascribing to him improbable, if not incredible, conceptions of himself? As was said at the end of the preceding chapter and will be said again in this, we can hardly account for the christological faith of the early Church without assuming the existence of something extraordinary in the consciousness of Jesus; and yet there are, as we have seen, sound grounds for doubt that he thought of himself either as the Messiah or as the Son of man or yet as the Servant. Can any more definite and positive statement on this point be made?

108

The Vocation of Jesus

I

Before undertaking, with very great tentativeness, such a statement, I should like to call attention again to a fact which has been dealt with earlier in our discussion and implied throughout, but which is particularly pertinent just now—namely, the amazing vitality and creativeness of early Christianity in the realm of ideas. We can easily set limits too rigid and narrow to "the power of his resurrection" (another way of referring to this vitality and creativeness) in this, as in other, realms. The Church's theology, particularly its Christology, was its attempt to explain and communicate the realities disclosed in its own existence. Now the Church was essentially a community of memory and the Spirit, and the miracle of its life was the realized identity of the Spirit with the remembered one. The event out of which the new society had emerged had happened around him, but it was also true that the new society itself now existed around him. "This Jesus hath God raised." (K.J.V.) The one who, living and crucified, had been the center of the event was now, raised and living, the center of the society. Jesus Christ was Lord. No wonder this became the creed or confession of the first Christians: it expressed the central existence of the Church.

But this apprehension of the identity of the Jesus whom they remembered with the Spirit whom they now knew—that is, this realization of the Resurrection—was an idea of enormous vitality and power. New ideas would have followed quickly in its train; old ideas would have been transfigured. Almost at once a whole new world of theological reflection would have been opened up. Since Jesus was the center and symbol of all that had happened and of all the Church essentially was, this reflection would inevitably have been concerned chiefly with him. Who was he that all of this should be true?

109

We cannot set limits to the Church's creativeness in answering this question. And it is important that we recognize both the impossibility of our doing so and the detraction from the "power of his resurrection" which is implicit in any attempt to do so.

Still, I repeat, when we ascribe the maximum degree of importance to this creativity, we yet find ourselves needing to affirm "something extraordinary" in the consciousness of Jesus in order to understand, as well as we can, the whole event. Besides—and much more important—this "something" belongs, I believe, to the Church's memory of Jesus himself. Any proposal to identify this element with precision and certainty would be intolerably presumptuous. But one who recognizes its presence is bound to make some attempt at describing it. My own attempt is made with full awareness of the hypothetical character of much that I shall say and with knowledge also that, even so, I have no really satisfactory solution to propose to the problem stated at the outset of this chapter. May we not say that even when allowance is made for differences in capacity for understanding among interpreters, such a solution is beyond the reach of any of us? Would we not agree, indeed, that the full recovery of the inner life of another person is impossible even in an ordinary case (if there is such a case) and where adequate source materials are available? But here we are dealing with what was certainly not an ordinary case, and our sources are meager and, for the most part, only indirectly relevant to our problem. In a word, although we cannot avoid the task of this chapter, we cannot hope really to accomplish it.

II

I have just said that the Gospels are largely irrelevant, or only indirectly relevant, to this task of trying to recover Jesus' sense of vocation. I had in mind the fact that the Synoptic Gospels, upon which we must chiefly depend for our knowledge of such a matter, throw little direct light upon the inner life of Jesus and indeed reveal little interest in that subject. It is true that the Fourth Gospel, if we could accept it as giving an accurate picture of Jesus and his human career, would tell us a great deal. We should then know that Jesus was deeply conscious of himself as being divine, that as the only Son he enjoyed uninterrupted communion with the Father, that he was aware of himself as coming from God and returning to God, that he remembered his life with the Father before the worlds were made. The texts of much of the teaching in this Gospel are great affirmations by Jesus of his own significance: "I am the light of the world"; "I am the bread of life"; "I am the resurrection and the life"; "Everyone who drinks of this water will thirst again, but whoever drinks of the water that I shall give him will never thirst"; "I and the Father are one"; and many more. But the very abundance of such passages in the Fourth Gospel makes more striking their almost complete absence from the earlier Gospels (the only real exception being Matt. 11:27-28 and its parallel in Luke). And since for the soundest historical reasons we must rely chiefly upon the Synoptic Gospels for the facts of Jesus' career, we must conclude that this kind of teaching was not characteristic.

It is true that hints or glimpses of what we may call the inner life of Jesus are constantly breaking through the prevailing objectivity of these Gospels, as in the recurrent phrase "moved by compassion," or in the way Jesus addresses God as "Father," or in occasional expressions of anger or of bitter disappointment or of ecstasy. Sometimes he is allowed to speak more directly about himself, as when he says, "Why do you call me good? No one is good but God." One remembers

111

also the poignant cry, "I have a baptism to be baptized with; and how I am constrained until it is accomplished!" as well as his prayer in Gethsemane and the "cry of dereliction" on the cross. But such passages, although they are incalculably precious (chiefly because they reflect his human sympathy, his human trust in God, his human feelings of perplexity, weakness, loneliness, and frustration) tell us little about his sense of vocation except (and even this quite indirectly) that it was a very exalted one and that he was profoundly committed to fulfilling it.

As a matter of fact the consciousness of Jesus, we are given every reason to believe, was not primarily a consciousness of himself. He was not preoccupied with his own status or "nature." His thoughts were turned, most of all, toward God— God's will so strenuously demanding, God's love so extravagantly bestowed, God's sovereignty so soon to be vindicated. His "self-consciousness" was predominantly the consciousness of being called to bear witness in deed and word to the kingdom of God—what it was and how near it was. Already it was beginning to be revealed. Already were the times being fulfilled. The glory of God, soon to be fully manifested, could already be discerned by those who had eyes to see it. He came preaching, not himself, but the Kingdom.

III

But all of this involves some thoughts about himself, and we cannot longer postpone some more definite suggestion as to the form his thoughts took. The general category which immediately presents itself is that of the prophet. The Synoptic Gospels often tell us he was thought of so by others: for example, "The multitudes . . . held him to be a prophet" (Matt. 21:46) ; "Others said, 'It is a prophet, like one of the prophets of old' " (Mark 6:15; also 8:28) ; "Fear seized them all; and they glorified God, saying, 'A great prophet has arisen among us!' " (Luke 7:16) . At least once disciples of Jesus described him so: "a prophet mighty in deed and word" (Luke 24:19) ; and twice Jesus is represented as using the term, by clear implication, of himself: "A prophet is not without honor, except in his own country" (Mark 6:4) and "Nevertheless I must go on my way today and tomorrow and the day following; for it cannot be that a prophet should perish away from Jerusalem" (Luke 13:33) . On the whole, it seems to me not unlikely that these indications and hints are true. Certainly, if a category must be found to which Jesus thought of himself as belonging, that of the prophet is the most likely, both a priori and on the basis of the Gospel evidence. I have already suggested that if he ever referred to himself as Son of man in a special sense, it may have been in the context of Ezekiel's use of that term.[1]

Actually, however, the evidence that Jesus applied the term "prophet" to himself is very sparse; and there is as little basis in the Gospels for holding that Jesus *claimed* to be a prophet as that he claimed to be the Messiah. Perhaps the real question is not whether he claimed to be a prophet, or indeed consciously thought of himself as being one, but rather whether his consciousness of God, of God's will, and of God's relations with men and more particularly with himself, was of the kind characteristic of the prophet. It seems to me highly probable that it was.

But such a consciousness, it must be vigorously affirmed, would not have precluded a sense of unique vocation, nor would it have implied any limit whatever upon the importance

[1] See above, p. 63. Also see C. K. Barrett, *The Holy Spirit and the Gospel Tradition* (London: S.P.C.K., 1947) , pp. 94-99.

of that vocation, except, of course, the limit involved in its being a human vocation. Every true prophet is aware of a unique calling. The word of God has come to him—to him uniquely and, in a sense, alone. No one else has heard just that "word" which he is to declare. And not only is he thus personally and uniquely *called;* he is, in some sense, personally and uniquely *possessed.* The principal mark of the primitive Hebrew prophets (the *nebiim*) was, of course, a kind of possession, manifesting itself in a suspension of the ordinary faculties and in the presence of strange and what could only be regarded as superhuman powers. Such persons belong to a well-recognized psychological type, the "ecstatic," which is both abnormal and pathological; and the greater Hebrew prophets, men of extraordinary intelligence and integrity, are not to be confused with these. Still, it is in the nature of the prophet to be ecstatic—to know the experience of being lifted out of himself and, in Paul's words (who was certainly one of them), to hear "things that cannot be told, which man may not utter" (II Cor. 12:4). This ecstatic power belongs also to the great poets, indeed to all persons of "genius." But it is the prophet who is likely to be most acutely aware of possessing it (or should we say, of being possessed by it?) because he is able most surely and clearly to identify the source of his inspiration. Inseparable from the prophet's ecstatic experience —indeed an essential element in it—is the assurance of the divine authority and the ultimate meaning and truth of it. It is the Most High God who has spoken—spoken not only *to* him, but now also *through* him. His words are not his own— they are God's—and yet in another sense they are most peculiarly his own, since God has spoken just these words through no one else. Manifestly there is no categorical limit to the range of this consciousness of God's activity. No one can say how high and deep it may be, how engrossing, or how pure and exalting. It is wrong, therefore, ever to say "only a prophet" or "just another prophet." No true prophet is just like another, nor can any arbitrary boundary be set to the depth of any particular prophet's sense of vocation or to the greatness of the work he believes God has given him to do.

But there is a special reason for avoiding these disparaging phrases when we speak of Jesus as a prophet. Franklin W. Young in a significant article [2] concludes that "in Jesus' day there were no Jewish prophets" and had not been for many generations. This may be an overstatement and has been challenged. For one thing, the apocalyptists were certainly prophets. The fact, however, that they wrote under ancient pseudonyms probably reflects, as Young points out, the current popular belief that the age of prophecy was in the past. Certainly it would have been said that the *great* age of prophecy was in the past. But Young shows that along with this belief that prophecy had ceased went the belief that it would be revived at the end of the age. The gift of prophecy was regarded as a mark of the messianic times. The appearance of a prophet would, then, have been an event of quite extraordinary significance. Note that in Luke 7:16 the people's exclamation, after Jesus' raising of the son of the widow of Nain, "A great prophet has arisen among us!" is followed immediately by "God has visited his people!"

Young goes too far, however, when he urges that the claim to being a prophet was tantamount to a messianic claim. It does not follow from the current belief that the messianic age would see the restoration of prophecy that anyone who felt

[2] "Jesus the Prophet: A Re-examination," *Journal of Biblical Literature,* LXVIII, 285 ff.

that he had received the spirit of prophecy would necessarily regard himself as Messiah, or even that others, recognizing the spirit of prophecy in him, would necessarily recognize him as the Messiah. As a matter of fact, the apocalyptists, although their adoption of the device of pseudonymity may be taken as evidence of the prevalent view that prophecy had ceased, must often have thought of themselves as prophets. But obviously none of them identified himself as the Messiah. Young's argument is based chiefly on the fact that, according to Josephus both Theudas and the unnamed Egyptian, who headed movements of revolt and thus conformed to the popular image of the Messiah, claimed to be "prophets." But actually we are not told that either Theudas or the Egyptian believed himself to be the Messiah, nor is there any indication that Josephus thought of them as making this claim. Indeed, in each case he seems to use the word "prophet" in the sense of "*a* prophet" (that is, the definite article is not employed): "Theudas . . . told them he was a prophet" and "the Egyptian . . . gained for himself the reputation of a prophet." [3] It is true that both of these men proposed themselves as leaders of rebellion against Roman rule, and at least one of them, Theudas, claimed that God would lend miraculous support to his effort. But all Zealots believed such things, and any Zealot leader might have made similar pretensions. We simply do not know the thoughts of Theudas and the Egyptian about messiahship and the Messiah. [4] We do not know whether they expected a Messiah,

[3] Josephus, *Antiquities* 20. 5. 1; *The Jewish War* 2. 13. 5.

[4] Neither Eusebius (*Church History* 2. 11) nor Acts (5:36; 21:38), our only other sources, adds to the information Josephus gives us in this respect. It is noteworthy that in the Jewish War of 66-70 there seems to have been no "Messiah," a fact pointed out by Lagrange, *Le Messianisme chez les Juifs* (Paris: Libraire Victor Lecoffre, 1909), pp. 25 ff.; and Manson, *The Servant Messiah*, p. 32. Because virtually our only source for this period of Jewish history is Josephus, we must be on guard, however, against hasty generalizations.

or how they thought of themselves as related to him if they did. All we can legitimately deduce from the data Young presents is that the appearance of a really impressive prophet in the time of Jesus, far from being a casual or ordinary thing, would have been interpreted by many as a sign of the coming Kingdom, and that any person who felt himself called to be a prophet would have known himself to stand in a relation of peculiar responsibility to the coming crisis. The nature of this consciousness would have varied greatly with every prophet, depending upon his moral and spiritual stature and his capacities for understanding, but there would have been no limit, except the human limit, to its depth and range.[5]

The fact that Josephus tells of no "Messiahs" does not need to mean that there were none. W. R. Farmer (*op. cit.*, pp. 11-23) shows that the Jewish historian was interested in representing the revolt of A.D. 66-70 as a merely political rebellion without real roots in the religious life and culture of the Jewish people. According to Josephus the war was *not*—as Farmer is sure it *was*—the culmination of a movement of religious nationalism which went back continuously to Maccabean times. If Josephus was thus biased, he may well have consciously avoided the term "Messiah," in connection with Judas, Theudas, the Egyptian, and the war itself. As Farmer points out, we do have references to various and apparently numerous Messiahs in the Gospels (see Mark 13:6, 21-22, and parallels in Matthew and Luke). It is interesting that in Mark 13: 22 (equals Matt. 24:24) mention is made of both "false Christs" and "false prophets."

[5] Mark 6:14-15 and 8:28, with contexts, indicate rather clear distinctions between the Messiah, the prophet (that is, Elijah), and "a prophet, like one of the prophets of old." It is possible that the whole matter of the role or office which Jesus thought of himself, and was thought of, as fulfilling will be greatly illumined by the Dead Sea Scrolls. Thus far the published materials do not greatly help in this particular respect, although they throw light on the origins and early history of the Church at other points. It may prove to be significant that the leader of the Qumran sect was known as "the Teacher of Righteousness" in view of the fact that Jesus was frequently addressed as "teacher." It is clear that the teacher of righteousness had, even during his lifetime, great authority among his disciples and that he was honored after his death. Cullmann writes: "But he died *as a prophet* [I do not know how technically Cullmann is using this word or what are his sources]. He belongs in the line of the prophets, who suffered as a *result* of their proclamation" ("The Significance of the Qumran Texts for Research into the Beginnings of Christianity," *The Journal of Biblical Literature*, LXXIV, 225) .

THE DEATH OF CHRIST

Jesus' consciousness of being a prophet would have been an aspect of his realization of the unique meaning of his times. He had been set in the midst of the great moment of all history and had been given to see its significance. Upon him had been laid the tremendous responsibility of declaring its meaning to all the nation. Just how he thought of himself as related to the coming crisis (and perhaps to the Son of man whom the crisis would bring), we do not know. One may wonder whether even he would have known. The greater the depth and mystery in Jesus' consciousness of vocation, and the more uniquely personal it was to himself, the less likely that he would have been able to define it. No traditional terms would have seemed appropriate to express it. No common vessel, however altered in shape, would have sufficed to hold his peculiar treasure. But his disciples would have been, however vaguely, aware of his sense of both the mystery of the Kingdom and the consequent mystery of his own relation to it.[6]

IV

This awareness, we may well believe, of the mystery of Jesus' vocation was never more real or acute among his followers than when he "set his face to go to Jerusalem" toward

[6] It may be argued that to recognize the presence in Jesus' self-consciousness of this mysterious element is to come very close to agreeing with those, mentioned earlier, who hold that Jesus had an entirely fresh conception of the nature and role of God's agent in the coming crisis (that is, neither "Son of man," "Messiah," nor any other traditional term was really appropriate) and that he thought of himself as being that person. This would be a more attractive view if it were not for the Gospel evidence that Jesus actually expected the Son of man. I should say that the question asked in Matt. 11:3 (equals Luke 7:19): "Are you he who is to come, or shall we look for another?" was a question raised for the early Church by many of Jesus' remembered teachings. And the answer to the question, it is important to note, was provided, not by any remembered *word* of Jesus, but by a recalling of his mighty works.

118

the end of his brief career. Mark may give us a true historical memory when he writes: "And they were on the road, going up to Jerusalem, and Jesus was walking ahead of them; and they were amazed, and those who followed were afraid." Jesus must have known that there was danger in going, that the popular following he had secured and the misguided enthusiasm of some of his disciples, not to mention the suspicion and enmity of powerful groups which he had incurred, exposed him to arrest. Except that he believed it to be the will of God, we cannot know just why he felt he must take these risks. It is usual to say that he was convinced that it was his duty to announce the coming Kingdom in his country's capital and to try to force a decision there for or against its demands. Such a motive might account for the public nature of his entry into the city (assuming that an actual intention of Jesus was expressed in the "triumphal entry") and for his act in purging the Temple. When it became clear (however soon or late) that his enemies were resolved and prepared to destroy him, we may be sure that he would have been preoccupied with the ordeal that confronted him. "I have a baptism to be baptized with; and how I am constrained until it is accomplished," may well be as authentic as it sounds. We can understand the foreboding with which he would have looked forward to his death, the inner struggle involved in accepting it; but we can understand also his having come to the conclusion that God would use even his death in bringing to fulfillment his sovereign purposes and that in that fulfillment he himself would share. There is no real evidence that he thought of Isa. 53 in that connection, but he would not have needed to suppose that *he* was the Suffering Servant, or even to have thought of the Servant as an individual at all, in order to have found light

119

and strength in this ancient scripture. We may surmise also, and with more evidence, that he meditated often on the significance of the fate of John the Baptist and the many prophets who for their fidelity in declaring the will of God had suffered torture and death. That in these last days he discussed his death with some of his disciples—that he sought to prepare them to accept it and to look beyond it—is altogether likely. How indeed could he have failed to do so, once the prospect became clear to his own mind? That Jesus' last meal with his disciples was darkened by the threat of his death, that Jesus acted out the parable of the broken body and the poured-out blood, that he said to them, "I shall not drink again of this fruit of the vine until that day when I drink it new with you in my Father's kingdom"—not only may it be said that all of this is credible, but one may also ask whether subsequent events would be understandable at all if all of this, or something like it, did not occur.

Another discussion of the issues we have considered in these four chapters speaks of the "raw materials of Christology."[7] This is an illuminating and useful phrase. Even if we are inclined to believe, as I am, that the Christian conception of Christ, his person and his "work," was the creation of early Christian reflection on the concrete realities of the event

[7] Fuller, op. cit., pp. 79 ff. This book, to which allusion has already been made, is both interesting and significant, although the author, I think, attributes to Jesus more definite ideas about himself and his death than the evidence justifies. In other words, it seems to me that the materials he finds are not "raw" enough. After my own book was completed and in the hands of the publisher, an article of great importance bearing on the theme of this chapter was presented by James M. Robinson in *Religion in Life* (XXVI, 40-49) under the title "The Historical Jesus and the Church's Kerygma." It seems to me that Robinson comes nearer than Fuller to pointing to really "raw materials of Christology."

and the Spirit in its own life—even so, the "raw materials" for this conception must have lain at hand. These would have included, of course, certain traditional categories of interpretation, such as Messiah, Son of man, and Servant of the Lord. But the *basic* "raw materials" would have been more concrete, consisting in actual memories of Jesus himself. There had been a mystery about him into which his disciples had never been initiated. He had had thoughts about himself which they had not been able to share. All who really knew him loved him, and some may have known and loved him well, but the knowledge was never complete familiarity and the love was not unmixed with awe. Only after the Resurrection were they able, as they thought, to understand this impression; but the impression itself was a matter of memory. Here, as at every other point, the remembrance of the man Jesus, no less than the experience of the risen Christ, participated as an essential element in the final creation of the Church's faith.

V

We began this section of four chapters on the perplexing problem of Jesus' thoughts about himself, his role, and therefore his death with the reminder that the problem is a problem for history, not for faith; and it may be well to conclude this part of our discussion with that same reminder. Much more important than the way one tries to solve the problem is the way one estimates the importance of the problem itself. As a matter of fact, if we view it as a problem vital to faith, it is unlikely that we can be disinterested enough to deal with it as what it is, a problem of history, and consequently unlikely that we shall be able to reach any kind of satisfactory solution. Even the *historical* importance of the problem is strictly limited.

The life of Jesus is the most significant life ever lived, but no more in his case than in that of any lesser figure of history does the truth of our estimate depend upon our finding that he himself placed the same value upon the significance of his career. The Christian faith is not a belief that Jesus entertained certain ideas, which therefore must be true; it is rather the conviction, grounded in the concrete realities of the Church's life (including the memory of Jesus himself), that his career was the central element in a divine and supremely significant event. That Jesus himself was sensitive to the uniqueness and urgency of the crisis in the midst of which he stood and to its divine meaning, we can be indubitably sure. And assurance on this point enables us to find a closer coherence and a deeper unity in the event than would otherwise appear. Indeed, it is hard to see how, without such awareness on Jesus' part, the event could have come to pass at all. But we do not need to go further and ascribe to him definite ideas about his own nature or office. Such ascriptions not only often fail to assist or support faith in Christ, they may even burden and obstruct it.

They have this adverse effect when they involve attributing to Jesus thoughts about himself which are incompatible with his full and unqualified humanity. For all his goodness and greatness, the wonder of his manhood, the qualities of mind and spirit which lift him so far above us, he was still a human being like ourselves. Not only should we not want it otherwise; we ought not to be able to bear it otherwise. Jesus was a man like ourselves; Jesus' nature was our common human nature. To say this is not to make a grudging concession to secular reason; it is to make a vital affirmation of Christian faith. We do well to speak of the humanity and the divinity of Jesus. But by his "humanity" we mean the whole nature of him who was "made like his brethren in every respect" (Heb. 2:17). The "divinity" was not half of his nature or a second nature, but was that purpose and activity of God which made the event which happened around him, but also in him and through him, the saving event it was. The divinity of Jesus was the deed of God. The uniqueness of Jesus was the absolute uniqueness of what God did in him.

III. THE CROSS
IN THE CHURCH

CHAPTER SIX

Center and Symbol

SINCE THE BEGINNING OF THIS DISCUSSION, WE HAVE BEEN MOVING toward "the center of greatest significance" in our theme; and now, in this and the following chapters, we actually touch that center itself. For it is the meaning of the Cross in the life of the Church and in the experience of the believer which is the really important thing, whether for the historian or the Christian man. We began by considering the death of Jesus in the perspective of the political situation in Palestine near the beginning of the first century. Later we were thinking about it as the culmination of his own singularly great and uniquely dedicated career. But not only may it be said that the death of Christ cannot be *adequately* seen in either of these contexts; one must also recognize that the death of *Christ* cannot be seen there at all. The death of *Christ* actually took place only in the context of an event which began (in the sense in which any event can be said to have a beginning) with the gathering of Jesus' disciples and ended (in the same approximate sense) with the creation of the Church, the new community of the Spirit, in which Jesus was remembered and was still known as the living Lord. The meaning of the Cross can be seen only in this context. Indeed, the Cross itself stands only there. For by the Cross we do not mean either the execution of a Roman political prisoner or the tragic end of a uniquely noble and devoted life. We mean the central moment in a divinely creative and redemptive event which only the Church remembers and the continuing meaning of which only the Church can know.

It goes without saying that an adequate or worthy discussion of so great a theme is hopelessly beyond our powers; but at least, we shall not be hampered by the methodological difficulty which has thus far beset our way. Up to this point we have been under the constant necessity of trying to distinguish between what may be loosely called the original facts and what the faith of the early Church may plausibly be thought of as contributing to the gospel story. But now this distinction becomes irrelevant. What we have in the Gospels are the words of Jesus and the incidents of his career as they lay in the mind and heart of the early Church, but it is precisely these words and incidents *thus oriented* in which we are interested. They *are* for our present purpose the "original facts." We do not have to isolate and exclude the contribution of early Christian life and faith (an impossible undertaking anyhow); on the contrary, we are seeking to give full place to this life and faith, understanding it not as something added to the event and to a degree distorting or obscuring it, but as part and parcel of the event itself. The intimate and inextricable involvment of fact and meaning, long recognized as characteristic of the Gospels, is now seen as characteristic also of the gospel. The fusion of history and interpretation, long thought of as an unfortunate entanglement of truth with error, must now be recognized as being itself the very reality we seek. It is on this account that the most profound critical study of the Gospels seems sometimes to bring us out near the same point to which a certain kind of devout naïve study also leads, and the scholar and the saint find themselves speaking the same language. The one has discovered what the other always knew—

that the gospel is not an inference or abstraction from the Gospels or a rationalization of them, but that the Gospels, just as they stand, contain it. To be sure, they are partly the product (as we say) of faith; but so is the gospel, and so was the event. And so, of course, was the Cross. But the Cross was not less real—or less really the Cross—because faith had a part in creating it. On the contrary, it had its own distinctive reality only on this account. The Cross *was* the Cross only in the context which the life of the primitive community provided.

I

In proposing to consider the meaning of the death of Christ within this life of the primitive Church, I do not have principally in mind the various so-called theories of the Atonement which the New Testament writers present. These, or at least some of them, will come in for some discussion in the following chapter. But even there we shall be primarily concerned with the meaning of the Cross in a more concrete, and I should say a more profound, sense than is represented by any "theory" or by all the theories together. What did the Cross of Christ *really* mean? What did the Cross really stand for, not in the thought of the primitive Church, but in its actual life.

Much too often we discuss the place of Jesus' death in the primitive faith as though it were primarily an object of thought. We attempt to account for the early Church's preoccupation with this theme—for the fact, for example, that Mark devotes almost half of his space to the Passion and the events presaging it—by pointing to how much of a problem the Cross would have constituted for the first believers in Jesus as Christ and Lord. It would have been at first a stumbling block and nonsense for them just as surely, and for the same reason, as it continued to be for outsiders, Jews and Greeks. How could

Christ have been crucified and still be Christ? How could one who had died so ignominiously be the Lord? The death would have stood squarely in the way of faith as an obstacle which must in some way be removed or got around. No wonder then, we often say, that the Cross became the object of so much attention. It was the principal theological problem confronting the early Church.[1]

But however true and pertinent this may be, it is obvious that such considerations are quite inadequate to account for the place of the Cross in the New Testament and in the community life for which it speaks. The death of Christ was, to be sure, a problem for faith (in the more intellectual meaning of that term); but it was also (in another and profounder sense) the very center of faith. Indeed, it could become so acute a problem for thought only because it was already so crucial a fact within the life of the community. It will not do to say that the Cross gained its place in the devotion of the Church as a result of the explanations of it which the early theologians worked out; rather, one must recognize that it was so important that the theologians should find adequate rationalizations of the Cross because the Cross itself stood at the very center of the Church's confessional life. The undertaking in this chapter is not to discuss these rationalizations but to consider the prior question. How can we describe and

[1] Davies (*op. cit.*, pp. 283-84), who is inclined to believe that the idea of a suffering Messiah belongs to pre-Christian Judaism, argues that what made the death of Christ an obstacle to faith, the *skandalon* of which Paul speaks in I Cor. 1:23 and elsewhere, was not the death itself but the shameful manner of it. This may be true for Paul, who had thoroughly assimilated the death within his religious life and thought, but I cannot believe that the death as such would not have been a stumbling block for Jewish hearers generally. That Jesus was put to death by crucifixion would only have accentuated the difficulty. By the time of the Fourth Gospel even the crucifixion has ceased to be an offense; it is the being "lifted up" of the Son of God.

130

understand the place of the Cross in the actual existence of the primitive community?

II

It must be recognized, first, that the death of Jesus was the actual center of the event to which the Church looked back in memory and in which lay the beginnings of its own life. It is of the nature of a historical event that no absolute lines can be drawn as to when it begins and when it ends except the limits of history itself. Within these limits, however, narrower definitions of an approximate sort are possible. Thus in the case of the event of Christ we can say that it began with the election of Israel as the people of Yahweh and will end with the full creation of the New Israel which Paul envisages in Rom. 11. Or we can say, with greater specification, that it began with the appearance of Jesus the prophet from Nazareth and his first disciples and ended with the gift of the Spirit and the emergence of the Church. But however we define it, the death of Jesus is its center. Now so far as history as a whole is concerned or even the history of Israel, this is a matter of faith—that is, it represents the way the Christian as such finds himself thinking. But as regards the event more narrowly and specifically defined, it is a matter of simple historical fact; the death of Jesus was, in the most literal sense, the center of the event. It is because this is a matter of fact that the centrality of the Cross in the larger context can be a matter of faith. The event obviously had two phases or movements—the death of Jesus unmistakably marks the point where the one has just ended and the other is about to begin.

The recognition of this position of Jesus' death within the event of Christ will prevent our denying to the historical career of Jesus the importance it actually possessed. If one knew only the epistles of the New Testament (with the possible exception of Hebrews) one might be in danger of supposing that the event of Christ—that is, the event in which the Church had its origin—could be defined even more narrowly than we have suggested, that it might be thought of as consisting only of the death and Resurrection. But one does not need to discover the Gospels, one has only to read more closely and reflectively the epistles themselves, to realize that this cannot be. The event, no matter how narrowly we attempt to conceive it, must be defined so as not only to include the earthly life, but to include it as of equal moment with all that followed upon it. The event had an essential structure; and in that structure the death stood, not at the beginning, but at the center.

This is true because it was the moral personality of Jesus and the character of his life as these were known and remembered which alone made the death significant and the Resurrection possible. My quarrel with some of the contemporary accounts of the contents of the primitive preaching is that they underestimate the amount of the attention which must have been given in it to the moral character of Jesus. The death was *Jesus'* death; the Resurrection was *Jesus'* resurrection; so that the question would always have been important: "Who was Jesus? What manner of man was he?" The very truth and appeal of the gospel depended upon its giving a true and impressive answer to this question. It is because that question was so important that we have the Gospel tradition at all. We must recognize, as we have had many occasions to remark, that this tradition contains much besides primitive memories of what Jesus actually said and did; it had been affected at every stage by the continuing experience and reflection of the churches. The consequent additions, amplifications, emendations, in its traditions the Church is able to recognize as such without loss; but it would never be possible for the Church to attribute the development of its whole tradition of Jesus' career to such a process of growth. It belongs to the very nature of the Church to know not only that Jesus lived but that *Jesus* lived. I mean that it is of the nature of the Church to remember a man who in word and act expressed that agape which later became the breath, the spirit, of the Church's life and which even then began to evoke a characteristic response. The Church trusts its memories of the man Jesus, not primarily because it believes the Gospel documents, but because it is itself the embodiment of the Resurrection and cannot deny its own life. The death and Resurrection, as their meaning is known within the Church, necessarily imply not only the fact of the historical life but also the quality of it as a life in which the agape which the community now knows as the essential principle of its own being began to be revealed.

The Resurrection, in other words, implies continuity as well as discontinuity with the human career that preceded it; and one can distort or destroy its meaning by neglecting either element. It is possible to make so much of the continuity that the Resurrection becomes hardly more than a resuscitation and therefore without radical theological significance of any kind. Those who insist upon the fleshly character of Jesus' resurrection body are doing this without knowing it. They do not see that the important question for faith is not the identity of the Jesus who ate with his disciples before his death with the Jesus who ate with them afterward, but rather the identity of this human Jesus with him who now makes himself known as the spiritual head of the Church and center of its life. If the Resurrection does not denote this latter identity, it has no great theological importance. It becomes a mere miracle like other miracles—greater perhaps, but not different—and the Ascension (or something else) must take its place as the really decisive moment for faith. I say, then, that to make too much of the continuity between the earthly human life and the resurrection life is to destroy the radical meaning of the Resurrection. But we are in greater danger perhaps of destroying that meaning in another way. We may so emphasize the *discontinuity* as that the death becomes the final end of an ultimately insignificant human career and the Resurrection the beginning of all that really matters in the event. If the one tendency has the effect of denying the true character of the Resurrection by discounting its decisive importance as marking an entirely new phase of the event, the other makes the same denial by lifting it out of the context of the event altogether. For the Resurrection is not only a real Resurrection (that is, it presupposes the real death), but it is the Resurrection of a real person (that is, it presupposes a vividly remembered individual). Although every part of the New Testament would affirm both of these facts, still it is perhaps true to say that the epistles tend to emphasize the discontinuity and the Gospels the continuity, and that therefore in this respect as in so many others they complement each other and exercise a mutually corrective effect.

III

One moves only slightly from this consideration of the death of Jesus as standing in the center of the event when one observes in the second place that the death was the focus of the Church's memory of the human career. Now this is a point which the New Testament itself does not make, at any rate explicitly; but not only can there be no doubt of its truth, but also, I am convinced, it is this simple and elementary fact which, more than any other, accounts for the importance of the death of Christ in both the devotion and the theology of the Church. One does not need documentary evidence, one has only to place oneself in the situation of Jesus' disciples, to know how intimately the remembrance of Jesus himself would have been associated in their minds with the remembrance of his death. It is not an accident that our family memorial days are always the anniversaries of death. The psychological reasons for this association we need not go into, although they are probably obvious enough; but the fact of it is familiar. The meaning and worth to us of another person are never so vividly clear as when he is taken from us, and at no other time are we so likely to see his life in its true character and its full range. This is true even of those we know only casually or by name. We quote lightly, often almost in jest, the proverb about the impropriety of speaking ill of one who has died; but the generally generous attitude we find ourselves taking toward the dead has a deeper basis than regard for conventional proprieties, or mere sentimentality, or even the realization that the dead can no longer injure or annoy us so that we can afford to be tolerant. This attitude is, certainly in part, a greater charity based upon a deeper understanding. It is not that one becomes blind to another's faults when he dies, or decides politely to ignore them, but that one sees them now in the truer, ampler context of our common humanity and, remembering one's own struggles and failures, is moved to sympathy rather than to censure. At the same time, what was really good in the other is allowed to make its true impression. But if this kind of thing can be said about the death of one whom we have known only casually, if at all, how much more can be said of one with whom we have been intimately associated and who has entered decisively and

135

creatively into making us the persons we are! The whole meaning of the other, his whole worth to us, comes home with almost unbearable poignancy. The bitter grief which death in such cases often brings us is owing not only to a sense of the finality and irreparableness of our loss, but also to the fact that we seem to realize for the first time, now when it is too late, how much we stood to lose, how much we once possessed.

Not only is it legitimate to invoke human considerations of this kind in our attempt to explain the centrality of the Cross in the life of the Church, I should say that it is absolutely necessary to do so. There is no possibility of our understanding it otherwise. To be sure, this involves the presupposition of a deep emotional response to Jesus on the part of his disciples—a matter concerning which the Gospels themselves are largely silent. These Gospels, generally speaking, present Jesus as the object of faith rather than of love. But there are occasional glimpses even there—especially in Luke and John—of the personal loyalty and devotion he evoked among those who knew him. And the love toward the risen Christ which is constantly implied and often expressed in the epistles, especially in the Pauline and Johannine epistles, points unmistakably to the existence of comparable feelings of loyalty among those who knew him in the days of his flesh. Here again the principle of continuity can be appealed to. The Church's devotion to Christ is a sequel to the disciples' devotion to their master. Not only must we assume, as we were doing a moment ago, that what the Church later knew as agape was already being manifested in the personal attitudes and behavior of Jesus; but we must also assume that this same agape had already begun to elicit its characteristic response among those who knew him. The Church, in other words, was already coming into existence. And if all of this is true, the death of

Jesus would have been the focus of the Church's attention, not at first for theological, but for obvious psychological, reasons. It was the event around which the whole remembered meaning of Jesus would inevitably have gathered. And the terrible circumstances of the death—the anguish of it, the ignominy, the violence and brutality of the means of it, the awful anomaly that one such as he should be made the victim of such cruelty and malignity—all of this would have had the effect of accentuating the emotional impact of the death and of making even more certain that thenceforth to remember Jesus was to remember first of all his Cross.

IV

One other factor, of an equally nontheological kind, contributing to this same effect needs also to be mentioned. This was the early Church's own liability to persecution. The violent death of Jesus was held the more vividly and centrally in memory because the same kind of violent death was a real and constantly present possibility for every Christian. To become a Christian was consciously to accept the threat of execution. One had become a witness to Christ; and the ultimate testimony, which might at any time be asked for, was the testimony of one's death. So the very word "witness" ($\mu\acute{\alpha}\rho\tau\upsilon\varsigma$) comes to mean "martyr." We are inclined to translate the Greek word now in one way and now in the other, even in the same context. Thus in Rev. 2:13 we are likely to render the term with "martyr" when it is being used of "Antipas . . . who was killed among you"; but in Rev. 1:5 and 3:14, where it is being used of Christ, to translate it "witness." But in all cases the same phrase is used ($\mu\acute{\alpha}\rho\tau\upsilon\varsigma$ $\acute{o}$ $\pi\iota\sigma\tau\acute{o}\varsigma$), and the meaning is essentially the same. Jesus had been the "faithful martyr." As the writer of the Pastoral epistles says, ". . . before Pontius Pilate [he had]

137

witnessed (μαρτυρήσαντος) a good confession" (I Tim. 6:13 K.J.V.) . The decision for Christ was a decision of readiness to share his martyrdom. Thus, one was "baptized into his death" in a much more stark and realistic way than we ordinarily have in mind when we read Rom. 6:3.

This element in the life of the early Church is likely to be ignored because the book of Acts gives so irenical a picture of the relations of Christianity and the state. It is commonly said that in the earliest period (roughly, before Domitian) the power of the Roman state was used for the protection and support of the Church (especially as against Jewish protests and attacks) ; that even after the turn of the first century, persecutions were infrequent and sporadic; and that it was not till late in the second century or even in the third that empire-wide efforts began to be made to destroy the Christian movement. There is, needless to say, a great deal of truth in this general picture. Certainly in the earliest period there was no organized, synchronized effort to liquidate the Church throughout the empire. Any prosecution of the Christians was conducted under local or provincial auspices.[2] But we must be on our guard against minimizing the prevalence, the frequency, or the severity of these persecutions. The fact that the surviving literary evidences of persecution in the first century are meager does not necessarily mean that the persecutions themselves were few and sporadic. We must also not fail to allow sufficiently for the manifest tendency of the writer of Luke-Acts to idealize

[2] We have reason to suspect that such prosecutions went on in Asia in the time of Domitian, and we know that they did in Bithynia-Pontus in the time of Trajan. In this same period Ignatius' letters let us see that the church in Syria was also being persecuted. An outbreak against the Christians in Rome in Nero's time is, of course, fully documented. And may not Suetonius' reference to the act of Claudius in putting down an uprising around a certain "Chrestus" point to something similar in an earlier period?

138

the relations of church and state in the primitive period. Mark, which dates from not later than A.D. 70, does not reflect a situation of peaceful coexistence! And if Christians were being called on to suffer for Christ at Rome (where Mark is usually placed), is it not likely that this was true elsewhere also? Certainly when I Peter was written "the same experience of suffering [was being] required of [the] brotherhood throughout the world" (5:9); why should we suppose that this was not true earlier? Paul tells of the several times he was beaten with rods (a Roman penalty); and it seems certain that his career ended in martyrdom, as apparently did those of Peter, James (two of them), and John. Paul also makes our sharing with Christ in his glory conditional upon our "suffering" with him (Rom. 8:17) and speaks of "peril, or sword" (Rom. 8:35) as among the trials of the Christians, continuing, "As it is written,

'For thy sake we are being killed all the day long;
we are regarded as sheep to be slaughtered.' "

In other words, throughout the empire from the very beginning the Christian was subject to the penalty of death—as a willful and persistent violator of the law against unlawful assembly, if on no other charge—and he might be called on at any time to bear his "witness," to make his "confession."

Frederick C. Grant closes his chapter on Mark's Passion narrative in his book *The Earliest Gospel* with these words:

The Christian martyrs in the Roman arena, in Mark's day, knew what the death of Jesus meant. They drank his cup—to its very dregs. And they likewise knew "the power of his resurrection." "They were put to death with exquisite cruelty," says Tacitus, "and to their sufferings Nero added mockery and derision. Some were covered with the skins of wild beasts, and left to be devoured by dogs; others were nailed to the cross; numbers were burnt alive; and many, covered with inflammable matter, were lighted up, when the day declined, to serve as torches during the night." These were the men and women who handed down the story of Jesus' death. . . . What it meant to them is probably something we shall never guess, unless we too stand someday in the same desperate place of utter need, and cry out for sympathy and compassion to One who himself faced all the blind, venomous hatred, the implacable, vindictive fury of brute, senseless power, and pray, with them and with the martyr Stephen, "Lord Jesus, receive my spirit." [3]

Is it any wonder that the Christians of this early period remembered Jesus' death, and remembered it as the central and decisive moment in the whole event?

V

In view of this centrality of the death within the Church's memory of Jesus and, somewhat more objectively, within the event itself, it is not strange that the Cross should have become the symbol of the whole meaning of the event. Almost at once, and with particular appropriateness, it would have become the symbol of the human career of Jesus—its character and its significance. Thus Paul can say to the church at Corinth, referring to his first visit there: "I decided to know nothing among you except Jesus Christ and him crucified." By "Jesus Christ" he means the risen one known within the experience of the Church; and when he adds "and him crucified," he alludes, not to the death alone, but to the whole historical career, for which the death so appropriately and impressively stood. The same meanings are involved when Paul, in the same letter, defines the gospel as the preaching of "Christ cruci-

[3] *Op. cit.*, p. 187. Used by permission of Abingdon Press.

fied." Indeed, if these two words "Christ crucified" do not
sum up and designate, respectively, the two phases or movements in the event—"Christ" standing for all that is involved
in the Resurrection, the Spirit, the new creation, the Church;
and "crucified" standing for the man Jesus, for what he did
and said and, mostly, what he was, and for the response many
made to him—unless the two words have some such inclusive
meaning, Paul's phrase is woefully inadequate.

More particularly the death would have suggested, symbolized, stood for, the whole concrete quality of Jesus' life, his
spirit, the agape which pre-eminently and essentially characterized him. This would probably have been true in any case,
for, as we have seen, the death of another is always likely to
have symbolic significance of this kind. But the fact that he
was put to death, and put to death so violently and brutally,
would have made such an appeal in his case both more sure
and more important. The callousness and cruelty of his cruci-
fiers would have set in even bolder relief the love which was
remembered as his distinctive spirit. His own grace and truth
would have shown more brilliantly because of the blackness of
the evil of which he was the victim. The very violence with
which his life was taken from him would have accentuated
the willingness he had always shown to lay it down. Indeed we
may well ask whether any dramatist or artist could possibly
have conceived in advance a more authentic or moving way of
exhibiting what we know as the spirit of Christ than this spectacle of his suffering in patience the agony of the Cross. Undoubtedly, as we have seen, the dramatic effects were heightened as the
story was told and retold. But history itself provided the essential theme. The author of the Fourth Gospel, himself a
dramatist of no mean ability, sees a certain providence in the
fact that Jesus was crucified (rather than being put to death in

some other way) : he was "lifted up" in his death. And so in fact he was. It is on the cross that he is most distinctly and most truly seen; it is on the cross that he draws us to him. The whole meaning of the man Jesus is, and has always been, indissolubly associated with the Cross. But because of the importance of this meaning within the event—the significance of the memory of the man within the life of the Church—it was natural that the Cross should have become the symbol, not of the man Jesus alone, but of the whole event of which his career was the center, and indeed of the whole redemptive purpose of God, who in Christ acted to reconcile the world to himself.

VI

Now it is in this context—the context provided by a recognition both of the actual centrality of the Cross within the event of Christ and of its symbolic power, that is, its power not only to recall the event to mind in a formal way, but also effectively to express and communicate its concrete meaning—it is in this context that all so-called theories of the Atonement must be considered. Far more important than judging among the several proposed theories, or even than knowing what they are, is recognizing what all these theories are really about. They purport to account for the centrality of the death of Jesus within the actual event, to set forth the important reasons why Jesus had to die. In fact, as I shall try to show in the following chapter, they represent various ways of trying to express the symbolic significance of the Cross and to communicate its symbolic power. They should be judged, not by their plausibility in accounting for the fact of Jesus' death as an incident within the event, but by their success in making clear and vivid authentic meanings of the event as a whole, of which that death proved to be the actual and symbolic center. Judged in the first way, all of the classical theories of the Atonement are false; judged in the second way, all of them are true. As I have said, it is not my intention to discuss with any thoroughness any of these conceptions.[4] I should like, however, to say enough about them to make clear the view of their nature and function which I have just expressed.

[4] This limitation in my purpose needs to be remembered. For a detailed discussion see Vincent Taylor, *The Atonement in New Testament Teaching* (London: Epworth Press, 1940). A most illuminating treatment of Paul's understanding of Jesus' death is to be found in Davies, *op. cit.,* pp. 227-84. This discussion bears on the ideas of other New Testament writers besides Paul and contains references to important literature.

CHAPTER SEVEN

Myths and Meanings

DISREGARDING MINOR VARIATIONS, ONE MAY SAY THAT THE NEW Testament presents two views of the purpose and effect of the death of Jesus, both of which have been held and variously elaborated in the subsequent history of the Church. A third view has emerged during the later period; but as we shall see, it implies one or the other of the original conceptions. The three conceptions may be designated for convenience in discussion by the terms "victory," "sacrifice," and "revelation," respectively. According to the first conception, Jesus' death represents the culmination of bitter struggle with the powers of evil, with sin and death, who held mankind in thrall. From this struggle he emerged the victor (witness the Resurrection), and thus delivered us from the power of our enemies. According to the second view, Jesus offered in his death an adequate sacrifice for sin, or in some other way atoned for sin, thus removing our guilt and effecting our reconciliation with God. According to the third, Jesus' death on the cross was for the purpose of providing that revelation of the love of God which would move us to repentance, evoke in us a responsive gratitude and loyalty, and thus deliver us from both our guilt and our bondage.

The third of these conceptions, I have just said, is not a characteristic New Testament idea. There is no evidence whatever that the early Church entertained the view that the purpose of Christ's death was to disclose the love of God. Indeed, there are surprisingly few New Testament passages which associate God's love with Jesus' death in any way at all. The most notable of these are: "As Moses lifted up the serpent in the wilderness, so must the Son of man be lifted up. . . . For God so loved the world that he gave his only Son, that whoever believes in him should not perish but have eternal life" (John 3:14, 16); "By this we know love, that he laid down his life for us" (I John 3:16); "In this the love of God was made manifest among us, that God sent his only Son into the world, . . . not that we loved God but that he loved us and sent his Son to be the expiation for our sins" (I John 4:9-10); and "God shows his love for us in that while we were yet sinners Christ died for us" (Rom. 5:8). But although all of these passages point to a revelatory meaning in the death of Christ— the death does disclose the love of God—that disclosure clearly lies in the realm of result rather than of purpose. There is no hint at all that the purpose of the death was to manifest God's love or that its effectiveness for our salvation lies in any degree in this disclosure. This revelation of love was an incidental consequence—an implication—of the death, not its purpose or even a part of its purpose. The Fourth Gospel, to be sure, often suggests that the purpose of Christ's coming was to reveal "the Father" or "the truth" and that salvation consists in "seeing" or "knowing" the reality he came to disclose. But there is no emphasis upon either the death of Christ or the love of God in this connection. The words of Jesus, "I, when I

145

am lifted up [in death] will draw all men to myself," stand alone in hinting at a connection between the Cross and revelation, but even these words do not suggest that what is revealed is the *love* of God. We must conclude that the so-called moral theory of the Atonement, classically expressed by Abelard and developed in various forms since then, cannot be traced to the primitive Church. This conception will be mentioned again later. But in this summary of New Testament teaching it has no proper place.

The other two conceptions, however—those of a victory won and of a sacrifice offered—belong to the very warp and woof of the New Testament. Thus Paul can speak of Christ's death as a "death to sin" (that is, sin is overcome) or as a "death for sin" (that is, sin is atoned for). He can speak of the death as having "canceled the bond which stood against us" (that is, a dealing with our guilt) or as having "disarmed the principalities and powers" (that is, a dealing with our slavery); as both a means of "expiation" and a "triumph" over the demons. He can speak of Christ both as having "bought" us "with a price" and as making us sharers in his own victory, both as having "become a curse for us" and as always leading us "in triumph." [1] Thus also the author to the Hebrews, who tells us that the purpose of Christ's coming was that "through death he might destroy him who has the power of death, . . . and deliver all those who through fear of death were subject to lifelong bondage," can in almost the same breath say that his purpose was to "become a merciful and faithful high priest . . . to make expiation for the sins of the people" (Heb. 2:14-17).

In the Fourth Gospel the death of Christ is pre-eminently a victory, a being "lifted up," a glorification; but even here

[1] See Rom. 3:25; 4:25; 6:10; I Cor. 6:20; II Cor. 2:14; 5:21; Gal. 3:13; Col. 2:14-15.

Jesus can be described as "the Lamb of God, who takes away the sin of the world!" (1:29). The Johannine epistles stress the expiatory significance of Christ's death with references to the "blood of Jesus" which "cleanses us from all sin" and to God as sending "his Son to be the expiation for our sins." So also does the writer of I Peter, who speaks of our being "ransomed" by "the precious blood of Christ, like that of a lamb without blemish or spot," and of Christ as having "suffered" for us and as bearing "our sins in his body on the tree." [2] But the one writer can say that "the reason the Son of God appeared was to destroy the works of the devil" (I John 3:8), and the other gives at least a hint of Christ's victory when he speaks of "angels, authorities, and powers" as "subject to him" (I Pet. 3:22). The author of the Apocalypse on the other hand characteristically sees Christ, not as a sacrificial victim, but as the victor who can say to his followers facing a martyr's death: "He who conquers, I will grant him to sit with me on my throne, as I myself conquered and sat down with my Father on his throne" (Rev. 3:21); still his favorite image for Christ is "the Lamb that was slain," and the martyrs are those who "have washed their robes and made them white in the blood of the Lamb" (Rev. 7:14). And whoever first said, "the Son of man must suffer" and combined the images of the triumphant Messiah of the Apocalypses and the Suffering Servant of Isa. 53 was only acknowledging and affirming these same two conceptions of the work of Christ. As Son of man he has overcome our enemies and set us free; as Servant he has atoned for our guilt and reconciled us to God.

Not only are these two conceptions everywhere to be found, often closely associated with each other in the same writer; but all the many ways in which the effectiveness of Jesus' death is

[2] See I John 1:7; 4:10; I Pet. 1:18-19; 2:21-24.

147

described in the New Testament, all the many images or metaphors employed, can be subsumed under one or the other of them. In view of the richness and variety of the New Testament teaching, generalizations of this kind are always dangerous, but this one can be made with assurance. Either Christ on the cross met and defeated the evil powers—especially sin and death—and thus delivered us from our enemies, or else he did what had to be done to atone for our guilt (whether thought of as paying a penalty or a debt or a ransom or as offering a cult sacrifice) and thus reconciled us to God. Actually he is thought of as doing both. He is both the conquering Son of God, who has seized the keys of death and hell, and the Lamb of God slain from the foundation of the world.[3]

[3] We may seem to be leaving out the idea of Jesus' obedience as the possible explanation of the efficacy of his death. Such an explanation may appear to be implied by Paul's statement (in Rom. 5:19) that just "as by one man's disobedience many were made sinners, so by one man's obedience many will be made righteous." Also in Phil. 2:8 Paul speaks of Christ's obedience even unto death as the ground of God's exaltation of him to be the Lord. A similar emphasis upon Jesus' obedience is characteristic of the Epistle to the Hebrews. I do not believe, however, that the recognition of this emphasis is inconsistent with the acceptance of the generalization I am defending—namely, that there are two overriding categories in terms of which the New Testament understands the effectiveness of the death of Jesus. Several things can be said about this obedience of Christ: sometimes it appears as the explanation of his willingness to suffer death rather than as an explanation of the intrinsic value of the death itself; and where it appears in the latter sense, it may be thought of either as breaking the power of sin and law (in which case, it belongs under "victory") or as making up in some way for our disobedience (in which case it falls in the general category I have labeled "sacrifice"). I have already referred to the admirable discussion of Paul's conception of the efficacy of Jesus' death in Davies, *op. cit.*, pp. 227-84. He makes a great deal of obedience, regarding it as "the essential category in Paul's understanding of the death of Jesus" and interpreting it in close connection with Jewish ideas of solidarity (especially under the Covenant) and the rabbinic conception of a treasury of merits. I do not regard anything in Davies' discussion as incompatible with the generalizations I have made thus far in this chapter, although I do feel that he slights somewhat the idea of victory. He does so perhaps because, as the title of his book indicates, he is interested particularly in points of contact between Paul and the rabbis.

II

Now neither of these conceptions will bear scrutiny if they are to be judged as ways of answering the historical question "Why was Jesus of Nazareth put to death?" or even the theological question "What did the death of Christ accomplish?" For one thing, each of them contradicts the other and belongs to an entirely separate realm of discourse. If the language of victory and sacrifice is taken literally and realistically, we might conceivably accept one or the other of the explanations, but not both. Actually, however, neither conception will really stand up, even by itself. The first, that of victory, reflects and necessarily involves a world view which modern men do not and cannot hold. We know, to be sure, the fact of human bondage. We recognize our condition as "slaves of sin" and as "subject to lifelong bondage" through the "fear of death." We are aware of our plight in the midst of mighty forces, biological and social, which divide us and threaten to destroy us, and which we seem helpless to control. In a word, we can sense, vividly enough, what the New Testament is talking about when it says that we "are not contending against flesh and blood, but against the principalities, against the powers, against the world rulers of this present darkness, against the spiritual hosts of wickedness in the heavenly places" (Eph. 6:12). But we are able to use such terms as these, even to find them indispensable, only because we take them metaphorically and symbolically. It is impossible for us to believe literally in the demonic hosts with their ruling princes. And although we will know that a real deliverance from the guilt and power of sin and the dread and doom of death has been offered us in Christ, we can hardly account for this fact by a personal victory of Jesus over the demonic powers—whether on the cross or anywhere else.

The second conception—the conception of the death as an adequate sacrifice for sin—is equally inadmissible as an explanation of this deliverance. Can we believe that God's grace needed to wait until such a sacrifice should be offered? If so, was it pure grace? Or that his forgiveness of us was dependent upon someone's paying the debt we owed? If so, can it be truly called forgiveness at all? And what realism can we attribute to these images of a sacrifice being offered or a debt being paid when it is seen that it is God himself who offers the sacrifice and pays the debt? I know that there are cruder and more subtle ways of stating this second conception. But if in however refined and sophisticated a way the death of Jesus is thought of as altering the objective situation of man vis-à-vis the righteous will of God, so that a "justification" is possible which could not have been granted otherwise, no matter what the subjective conditions—if the death is so thought of, these difficulties cannot be avoided and are, in the last resort, insuperable. Either we take literally and realistically the view that Jesus' death made a difference of this kind, in which case we cannot avoid a reflection upon the love of God and the personal character of his relations with us; or else we recognize, with the New Testament, that it is God who in Christ is reconciling us to himself, in which case we are bound to reject the forensic or juridical conception of the effect of Jesus' death.

But the third conception, often called the "moral theory" of the Atonement, which finds that the purpose of the death was to make known the love of God, must also be rejected if what we are seeking is an explanation of the "why" of Jesus' death. For how could the death have had this effect if something more objective was not also being accomplished through it?

The death must benefit us if it is to reveal love for us. It will not do to say that it benefits us because, or in the sense that, it reveals love. That would be to argue in a circle. It has to be recognized as benefiting us *before* it can be recognized as expressing love. Implicit, then, in the "moral theory" is the acceptance of one of the other two conceptions. Either Jesus in his death at great cost to himself won a victory on our behalf over the evil powers, who held us helpless in their grip, or else at the price of the same suffering he satisfied in some way the demands of the law which stood inexorably against us and which we were helpless to fulfill. In either case the death would become a moving exhibition of love—of the love of Jesus if not of God—but we have already observed the difficulties in the way of the literal acceptance of either of these conceptions.

III

What are we to say, then? Are the conceptions to be rejected as unilluminating and untrue? By no means. They are both illuminating and true, and belong so profoundly and universally to the Church's tradition and life that they cannot be, will never be, rejected. But they are illuminating and true, not as theories of the Atonement, not as rational explanations of the fact of Jesus' death, but being taken much more concretely, as dramatic ways of expressing meanings of the whole event of Christ, of which the death is, as we have seen, both the actual and symbolic center.

I have said that the two conceptions are logically contradictory. So they are; but there is also a certain logical necessity about them, for they answer to the two ways in which our human need of salvation is bound to be felt. That need will manifest itself, existentially or from within, as a need for deliverance from the Evil which has mastered us, and for reconciliation with the Good, from which our own sinful acts have estranged us. As helpless sinners (which we are) we need *deliverance*. As responsible sinners (which we also are) we need *forgiveness*. This is our existential situation, and the New Testament doctrine of the work of Christ answers to it. When our plight as slaves of sin, helpless victims of demonic powers, is at the center of attention (as it is, for example, in the latter part of Rom. 7), the work of the Savior must be thought of as an act of victorious struggle and mighty deliverance. But when sin appears, as it more often does, less hypostatically or personally, as rebellion against God or the violation of his will, then the act of the Savior becomes necessarily an act of expiation (or, in some sense, propitiation) and therefore of atonement.

It may be noticed, in passing, that this same duality in our existential need accounts for the two ways—and, again, the quite contradictory ways—in which law and death are looked at in the New Testament. The ambiguity, or ambivalence, at each of these points appears most clearly in Paul; but there are hints of it elsewhere, and it is implicit in the whole New Testament understanding of the human situation. Paul can say that the law is "holy and just and good"; but he can also speak of it as "the power of sin." It is both the gift of God and one of the enemies (along with sin and death) from which we need to be delivered. One cannot find such statements logically compatible; but one must see that each belongs logically—indeed by a kind of necessity—within its own proper context. If our situation is being thought of as that of bondage to sin, then law appears as the ally of sin, an evil and hostile thing. If, however, our position as responsible violators of God's will, as guilty before him, is being considered, the law is seen as *his* law, given us in his mercy to warn and convict us. In the same way, death appears in the New Testament both as "the wages of sin" and a judgment of God. C. H. Dodd in his commentary on Romans [4] tries to interpret "the wrath" in Paul as being a purely objective thing. It is not, he says, "the wrath of God" in any personal sense; this phrase is found, to be sure, but it is a mere vestige of an earlier view. The "wrath" is, rather, a kind of inevitable, almost automatic, consequence of sin. Sin *works itself out* in death. But actually there is no way to eliminate the evidence that Paul also thought of death as a punishment of sin and of "the wrath" as the righteous judgment of God upon those who have disobeyed his will. Both ways of regarding death are found; neither can be got rid of, nor can they be made logically compatible with each other. But again, although each contradicts the other, it belongs logically within its own appropriate structure. If sin and law are being thought of as demonic powers from which we need to be delivered, death appears with them as the most hateful and powerful of them, our "last enemy." If sin is being thought of as our responsible violation of God's holy law, then death appears as his judgment upon our disobedience.

In other words, we have in the New Testament two "stories," two dramatic representations of existential man and his redemption. Each story is coherent and consistent in itself, and each story is profoundly true; but the two stories cannot be mixed, with anything like a logically coherent result. In both stories Man, Sin, Law, Death, and Christ appear. But the role which each plays varies with the story. In the one, Man is the helpless slave of Sin, who uses the Law to keep him in subjection and finally rewards his victim by turning

[4] New York: Harper & Bros., n.d.

him over to Death. In this story Christ appears as the Conqueror of Sin, Law, and Death. In the other story, man has sinned against God's holy law and has incurred the penalty of death. In this story Christ appears as the justifier, the reconciler, the "means of expiation" or in some similar role. We often hear of "the drama of salvation"; actually there are two dramas. And moreover, there *must* be two dramas if the meaning of the salvation is to be adequately set forth.

The meanings, then, which the images victory and sacrifice were created to express were empirical meanings. They were realities known, at least in principle or in their first fruits, within the life of the Church, and among those who participated in the Spirit. One of these was the reality of deliverance from sin, emancipation from its power, a dying to the world and therefore a wonderful release from bondage to the fear of death, a new hope, based on an actual foretaste, of the life everlasting. The realization of this deliverance belonged, and of course belongs still, to the very existence of the new community of the Spirit. No ordinary terms could express or convey the meaning of this experience. The bitterness, the hopelessness, of the bondage, and the wonder of the release both beggared mere description. And so there came into being—almost as a part of the event itself—the story of God's sending his own Son into the world to meet our enemies of sin and death, of his struggle with them, of his victory over them. This story is not only true; it is indispensable and irreplaceable. But it is true and irreplaceable, not because it explains, in a causal or instrumental sense, the deliverance which God through Christ makes available to us, but because it conveys something of the concrete meaning of the deliverance, its quality and its transforming power, and because that quality and that power can be conveyed in no other way.

But involved in, or with, this deliverance from bondage was also a realization of forgiveness, of release from guilt, of a new peace with God, of reconciliation with him and therefore with others and with ourselves—in a word, of atonement. This experience, too, called for description but beggared any descriptive terms. How could so deep an estrangement have been so completely overcome? How could forgiveness be so full and free when our guilt is so great and our love of God is so fitful and unfaithful? How can it be that God, who is holy and cannot pass over sin, has yet forgiven us—that whereas I know myself forgiven, I know also that the full enormity of my sin has been seen and reckoned with? In view of the grossness of my offense, how could grace be so true and truth so full of grace? How could mercy be so just and justice so merciful? It was not a matter of proving the existence of this kind of forgiveness in the early Church—that was a known, a given fact—nor yet, in the first instance, of theoretically understanding it, but of describing it and communicating the concrete meaning or quality of it. And here again a story proved the only possible way. Just as the ancient Hebrew could express his insight into man's nature, with its awful contradictions of evil and good, only with the story of the Creation and the Fall, so the early Christians could express the true inwardness of their situation as forgiven sinners only with the story of the sinless Son of God, who suffered death upon the cross for our transgressions and in our stead. And just as the biblical view of man, in its concreteness and particularity, can still be expressed and conveyed only through the ancient myth of Eden, so the image of "the Lamb of God, who takes away the sin of the world" is inseparably associated with the distinctively Christian experience of forgiveness.

We see, then, that both the images of Christ the victor over

the demons and of Christ the Lamb of God are true and indispensable. They are true, because they answer to, recall, actually
recreate, real and essential elements in the concrete meaning
of the event and the life of the Church. They are indispensable
because—for historical reasons, if for no other—they alone
can do this. To describe the salvation in Christ without the
use of these two images and the stories to which they belong
is impossible; one would be speaking of some other salvation
or of no salvation at all. Different as they are—even contradictory, for how could the Victor be also the Lamb?—they
are true in the way two very different portraits of the same
person can be true or two very different poems inspired by
the same scene or event. But these analogies only partly hold,
for there is an inevitability, a kind of necessity, about the two
images that are being discussed which no particular portrait
or poem can claim. They belong essentially and ineradicably
to the life of the historical community, being so deeply em-
bedded in its life that they may be thought of as creations,
not of individual Christians or even of the community as a
whole, but of him who moved through the ancient event to
bring the Church itself into being.

IV

But the Church's knowledge of the victory and the forgiveness which God made available in Christ does not follow upon
its acceptance of the truth, in any sense, of these images, although that knowledge is, as has been said, intrinsically and by
a kind of necessity, bound up with them; rather, the images
depend upon the knowledge. The knowledge does not follow
upon the belief that the ancient myths are true; rather we
find the myths meaningful and true because the knowledge
is given independently of them, although inseparably with

them. The knowledge is given with membership in the Church, with participation in the memory and the Spirit which together constitute and distinguish the Church. It belongs—as the myths also do but in a prior sense—to God's new creation.

This new creation was brought to pass through an event in our history at the center of which stood the Cross of Christ and at the center of our memory of which the Cross still stands. Because of that actual centrality the Cross is a symbol of the whole meaning of the whole event; it was not, as an incident in the career of Jesus, the effective cause or source of that meaning. We may well say that, so far as we can see, the event would not have had its characteristic effect had it not been for the death of Christ—but that is true only because it would not have been, in that case, the particular event it was. That this event had the particular result it had—a new community in which are found a new forgiveness, victory, and hope—is a matter of empirical knowledge in the Church; but why this particular event had this particular result is a matter altogether beyond our knowing. God's thoughts are not our thoughts, and his ways are not our ways. The event was a whole event, and its effect was a whole effect. We cannot break the event into parts and attribute the whole effect to one part, nor can we ascribe any particular part of the effect to any particular part of the event. Both event and effect are one and indivisible; and moreover, they belong indissolubly together. Of this whole the remembered death of Jesus is the poignant center. And the death of the Son of God is the all but inevitable symbol of its ineffable meaning.

CHAPTER EIGHT

The Cross and the Christian Way

IN THE TWO PRECEDING CHAPTERS AN ATTEMPT HAS BEEN MADE to state the theological meaning of the Cross—how it became for the Church the symbol of the whole event of Christ and of all the values that event had proved to have. But besides thus standing for the entire event and its meaning, the Cross has always represented more pointedly, and with particular appropriateness, a certain quality of what may be called the Christian way. I have in mind especially the related and inseparable convictions that the way of Christ is a way of love, that this way must be followed at the cost of whatever suffering, and that the suffering thus incurred, and indeed all suffering patiently borne, can have redemptive meaning. Our discussion of the place of the death of Christ in the life and faith of the early Church would not be even summarily complete if it did not include some recognition of this aspect of its meaning.

I

We have seen that the so-called "moral theory of the Atonement"—the view that the efficacy of the Cross lay in its being a revelation of the love of God—was not a characteristic New Testament idea; and moreover, that it cannot be rationally defended as an explanation of the "why" of Jesus' death. We saw that the death of Christ could not have had the effect of revealing God's love for us unless it also, and first, had accomplished something more objective in our behalf. We saw that this "something more objective" was conceived of in the early Church as either the winning of a victory over sin or the providing of a means of expiation for sin, or as both; but that these ways of explaining the "why" of the Cross are as incapable of being defended rationally as is the other. Our conclusion was that the saving effect we are seeking to account for with our "theories" was the effect of the whole event, not simply, or even chiefly, of the death; and that though there can be no doubt, from the Christian point of view, that a great deliverance and a great reconcilation were accomplished, we cannot hope to know just why this particular event had this particular effect. We recognized that actually the cause must lie, not within the event at all, but in God, who moved through it. The event was the saving event, not because of any particular feature of it or element in it, but because in it God "visited and redeemed his people."

To say this, however, is to say something, not merely about the effect of the event, but also about its basic character and, indeed, about its purpose insofar as we can know it. The event was the medium of God's drawing near to us. It was therefore— the whole event, it must be remembered, not the death only or particularly—the locus of the revelation of God's love. Let it be noted, however, that "revelation" must now be thought of as meaning, not the mere imparting of the truth about a reality (as in the "moral theory"), but the actual presence and activity of the reality itself. In Christ—that is, in the entire event—the love of God was not simply made known, as a fact is made known to our understanding; it was actually "poured into our hearts" (Rom. 5:5). When we speak of

God's love, then, we are speaking of more than the motive which lies back of God's saving action and is disclosed in it; we are speaking of the saving action itself. The love does not merely *account* for our redemption; it *is* our redemption. It *is* the very reconciliation we need—with God, with others, with ourselves. It *is* the very victory we need—over our pride, our self-concern, our fear. The central meaning of the event was, then, the coming into our history of this love. The central meaning of membership in the Church was participation in this love. As is true of "reconciliation" (or "atonement") also, agape is a way of referring to the essential existence of both the Church and the event. If the disclosing of the fact of God's love is proposed as the deliberate purpose of the death, the proposal must be rejected. If, however, the actual outpouring of the reality of God's love is proposed as the essential meaning and effect of the whole event, no proposal could be more fully and manifestly true.

But although the death of Christ cannot be cited as the reason why the event had this character and effect, it was inevitable, as we have already briefly noticed, that in becoming as it did the symbol of the entire event, it should become in a special sense the symbol of this essential meaning. That though innocent Jesus bore the cruel punishment without bitterness; that though reviled, he reviled not again; that though he suffered, he threatened not; though he endured such hostility of sinners against himself, he did not render evil for evil or railing for railing, but contrariwise blessed his persecutors— this is one of the most manifest and persistent meanings of the Cross. The King of love patiently suffering the ultimate in pain and shame! The one not only perfectly innocent but also perfect in goodness become the helpless and unprotesting victim of the most fiendish evil! No wonder the early Church,

160

as we have seen, unable to bear so terrible a contradiction, was forced to say, "He hath borne our griefs. . . . He was wounded for our transgressions. . . . The chastisement of our peace was upon him. . . ." (Isa. 53:45 K.J.V.) No wonder the Cross became the supreme symbol of the outpoured love of God!

But it became also almost at once a symbol of the Christian way—that is, of the Christian life not only on the more passive side as a grateful receiving of this love, but also, and in the more active sense, as the realization of obligation to express it in one's attitudes and conduct toward others. The Cross became a symbol of the Christian's duty as well as of God's gift. This meaning of the death of Christ is perhaps most explicit in I Pet., from which some of the familiar phrases in the preceding paragraph were drawn. The letter is rich in teaching of this kind. Speaking to the slaves in the several congregations he is addressing, the writer says: "What credit is it, if when you do wrong and are beaten for it you take it patiently? But if when you do right and suffer for it you take it patiently, you have God's approval. For to this you have been called, because Christ also suffered for you, leaving you an example, that you should follow in his steps." (2:20-21.) The same appeal to the example of Christ's death is made in 3:14 ff., where again the writer is urging that "it is better to suffer for doing right, if that should be God's will, than for doing wrong"; and toward the end of the epistle, after referring to the prospect of a "fiery ordeal," he says: "But rejoice in so far as you share Christ's sufferings." Paul also can speak about how we "suffer with him" (Rom. 8:17) and mentions the "death on a cross" as the climactic manifestation of that sacrificial "mind" which the Christians at Philippi are called upon to express toward one another (Phil. 2:5-8). There are those who argue that the Gospels, especially Mark, are under one of their most important aspects early martyrologies—that is, they are accounts of Jesus' martyrdom designed to encourage Christians to bear their own sufferings firmly and patiently even unto death.[1] And the connection between Christ's death and the Christian's call to self-abnegating service is made quite explicit in such teachings of the Gospels as "If any man would come after me, let him deny himself and take up his cross and follow me" (Mark 8:34), and "Whoever does not bear his own cross and come after me, cannot be my disciple" (Luke 14:27).

II

The Cross, then, stands for the entire Christian way of looking at and living life. It is the real crux of decision for or against Christ. One can do three things with the Cross—and only three. One can deny that it happened because, if acknowledged, it would make nonsense of life; one can acknowledge it and decide in consequence that life is meaningless; or one can find in it a clue to a deeper meaning in life than otherwise appears. There are no other possibilities. Without leaving the New Testament, may I conclude these chapters by discussing briefly these three possible positions as they confront us in our own world and challenge our own personal decision?

The simplest, most comfortable, and most obvious thing to do about the Cross in this sense is to deny that it happened, or—what is the same thing—forget that it happened or ignore that it happened; for there is more than one way to deny the reality of the Cross. Indeed, it is because of the ease with which we can avoid the terrible contradiction which it involves that Paul was resolved to know at Corinth nothing else but "Christ crucified" (there we have the contradiction stated

[1] See D. W. Riddle, *The Martyrs* (University of Chicago Press, 1931), pp. 180-218.

in the two essential words) and that in his preaching among the Galatians he saw to it that Jesus Christ the crucified should be "placarded," as he says, before their very eyes. Someone has said that it would be impossible for us to bear the sight of an absolutely blameless person in pain, having in mind, I would suppose, not our humane sensitiveness to the pain of others which a recognition of their demerit would render more tolerable, but rather the shattering effect of such a spectacle upon our whole world of values. Paul is amazed that having seen Jesus Christ crucified, any of the Galatians should have still intact their neat systems of legal *quid pro quo's*. Manifestly they have not seen him crucified. But how, Paul asks, could they have failed to see what he had so plainly and publicly portrayed? They had not seen because they did not want to see; or if they had once seen, they had forgotten because they wanted to forget. After all, how could they bear the world if they did not believe that those who rejoice deserve to rejoice and those who suffer deserve to suffer? How could they afford to put anywhere near the center of their world view the spectacle of a perfectly good man suffering the extremes of agony of flesh and spirit? Or how could we? What would happen to the order and security of our familiar world if we did?

I say there is more than one way to deny the fact of the Cross. One does not need explicitly and formally to deny that the crucifixion of Jesus occurred under Pontius Pilate; that fact is too well established to be doubted. One has only to think of Pontius Pilate, Jesus, and all the other participants as belonging to a kind of special world of their own, a kind of sacred wonder-book world remote from ours. To think thus is very easy; indeed, it may be quite difficult to think otherwise. The ineffable meanings found in the event, about which we were

thinking in the preceding chapter, the mythological creations
in which these meanings were expressed, tend to change the
history itself into story. Besides, it all happened so long ago
and so far away, and things were so different then. And Jesus
was not really a man—that is, in the sense in which we are
men—and his enemies were not real men, either. They were
all actors in a kind of drama, the original Passion play. The
events of his life and death were not part and parcel of the
history we belong to. They were a kind of miraculous insert.
After all, Jesus lived in a very special world—where angels
are seen, and heavenly voices are heard, where five buns can
feed five thousand families with much to spare, where the sea
can sometimes be walked on, and dead men can on occasion
come alive again and be restored to their families—Jesus'
world was not our world; and it was in that world, not ours,
that the cross stood. The "green hill" is "far away" indeed.
So far away that its shadow does not fall athwart our customary
ways; it holds no threat to the familiar and comfortable struc-
tures of our world. It happened, yes, but it happened in its
own special history, and therefore it did not really happen at all.

But if some of us deny the Cross in order to be able to
believe in life—that is, in life as we want to believe in it—
others acknowledge the Cross and deny the meaning of life;
or perhaps better, we all at different times and in different
moods do both. This denial of the meaning of life may take
the form of bitter resentment or of cynical aloofness. But it
stems from a recognition of the undeserved and apparently
useless and purposeless suffering in the world. Here is the
principal source of modern skepticism and atheism. Sometimes
we attribute the theological unbelief of our age to the evolution
of the scientific world view. That has undoubtedly contributed,
as have many other factors. But the decisively important factor

is what Studdert-Kennedy called the crucifixion in our street, the recognition that has been forced on even the least discerning of the appalling fact and proportions of undeserved suffering.

If we could acknowledge many gods or several, as the ancients could, we should undoubtedly find it easier to acknowledge God at all. We might then confine the responsibility of *our* God to some particular segment or phase of our experience and leave the rest to other gods. But this we cannot do. Modern man must make his choice between one God or no God at all. Ancient man had an easier option. Theism is native to man, but the naïve theism is not monotheism. Polytheism is the naïve faith, for it is able most readily to take account both of the manifest presence of the divine in human life and, at the same time, of the diversities and contradictions it contains. There would be no hesitation about acknowledging God— indeed, we could hardly help doing so; the divine actually hedges us about and all but forces itself on our attention— if we did not have to acknowledge him as *one* God. Who has not heard the heavens telling forth God's glory or glimpsed his form walking upon the wings of the wind? Who has not felt the portent of a divine judgment in the earthquake, the storm at sea, or the exploding bomb? Who needs to be told that duty is the "stern Daughter of the Voice of God"? Who has not felt the mystery of love as a holy miracle or found communion with a friend suddenly become a sacrament? Who has not had "thoughts that do often lie too deep for tears" in the presence of some common thing become for a moment un- bearably shining and eloquent? No, God is as certainly in- escapable in modern as in ancient times. The difference is that we, to acknowledge God, must acknowledge one God; and therefore, while the numinous in our experience says Yes, the contradictions within it say No. Wordsworth is think-

ing of this difference when he concludes his familiar sonnet
on our dullness to the glory in nature:

> For this, for every thing, we are out of tune;
> It moves us not.—Great God! I'd rather be
> A Pagan suckled in a creed outworn,—
> So might I, standing on this pleasant lea,
> Have glimpses that would make me less forlorn;
> Have sight of Proteus rising from the sea;
> Or hear old Triton blow his wreathèd horn.

Better have many gods than none at all. But the fact is that
polytheism *is* a "creed outworn." For whatever reason, we
are intellectually surer that God is one than that he is. And the
principal reason for our doubt is the Cross—not the Cross on
Calvary only, but that Cross as a symbol of the undeserved
and unrequited agony which we visit, or see visited, on others
and perhaps may sometimes suffer ourselves.

I remember many years ago spending a particular morning
reading Sir James Jeans' *Mysterious Universe,* a book in which
he gave some suggestion of how completely modern physics
had demolished the earlier mechanistic conceptions of Newton
and Darwin and in which he cited evidences of what he
called a cosmic mind. I recall still the elation with which I
laid the book down. At last science, which had seemed to many
in my generation the great enemy, was upholding the hands
of faith! But on that same afternoon I visited an old man
who lived scarcely two blocks from my home. He was completely blind and lived alone and forsaken in a small basement
room not more than eight feet square. In the room were a
single broken chair, a tiny stove, and a narrow cot without
sheets and covered only by several very dirty and threadbare
blankets. Over the bed nailed to the wall was a vessel in which

I caught a glimpse of some scraps of soiled bread. When I entered on that December day, he was gropingly trying, without either wood or fresh coal, to rekindle the almost dead embers of his fire. And my elation vanished. I realized that here was a more eloquent argument against the love and justice of God—and therefore of his existence in any sense that mattered —than ever was written in a book or spoken from a platform, and an argument which no scientist or theologian could adequately answer. What mattered the cosmic mind if there was no cosmic heart?

And so there are many—and who of us will say that he is not at certain times and in certain moods among them—who, unable to deny the fact of the Cross, deny rather the meaning of life.

But there is a third way, a way of acceptance of both the Cross and life. I say "of the Cross and life" as though two things were involved; but really there is no way of accepting the Cross except as a part of life or of rejecting life without also rejecting the Cross, and there is no way of denying the Cross without denying life. I said that the first position denied the Cross in order to accept life and that the second accepted the Cross though it meant denying life. But this is not really true. Neither the conventional moralist or rationalist, nor yet the cynic, really accepts either the Cross or life. Both ways are ways of rejection. If the conventional moralist rejects the Cross of Jesus by confining Calvary to the pages of a storybook, he also rejects life by closing his eyes to the continuing Gethsemanes and Golgothas—to what is still being done to God's little ones. The present world without the Cross is as much a dream world as any ancient world could be, with all its mysteries and miracles. And though the cynic may acknowledge the fact of the Cross, he does not really accept the Cross itself, for he sees it only as an evil and destructive thing. It is only one who sees the Cross as transforming and redeeming life who can really accept either the Cross or life.

But what does the acceptance of the transforming Cross mean? It means, for one thing, recognizing that there is a higher and deeper dimension in human life than either law can define or reason grasp, that both evil and good are deeper mysteries than we shall ever in this life understand and more potent forces than we shall ever be able to control. The stake on Calvary points in two directions—to abominable depths of evil, which we can never measure with our science or restrain with our rules, and to a goodness as far above us as the skies. If demonic evil is to be conquered, only divine goodness can conquer it; and the Cross, set within our history, is the point of the meeting and the struggle. Accepting the Cross does not mean understanding it; it means almost the contrary—recognizing a dimension and a potency in human life which defy our comprehension and all our little systems, whether of law or truth.

It means also recognizing, again without understanding, that God's love is somehow able to manifest itself in and through suffering as in no other way; that the evil in human life, which, as we have seen, constitutes the decisive argument against God's reality, also gives God his supreme opportunity to manifest his reality; that what at one level amounts to a denial of the meaning of existence, at a deeper level becomes the ground of the only possible faith in that meaning. The very contradiction which at first says No later says, "But it must be," and finally, "It is." Why should it be that one cannot really accept suffering—that is, with humility, patience, and courage—without finding it a way to God, or rather a way of God to us? Or how does it happen that we cannot witness another suffering unjustly, but in love, without feeling that somehow he is suffering for us? Why should such a spectacle move us to faith and contrition as nothing else can do? I shall not try to say why these things should be or how they can be, but who will deny that they are so? Jesus said from the cross, "Father, forgive them"; and who will count the millions who have been forgiven because he did—forgiven because the spectacle of his suffering has led them to repentance? Such love, thus lifted up, does draw all men.

Does it seem that after rejecting the "revelation" theory of the Atonement, I am now assuming it? Actually, I am not. I am not trying to explain why Jesus died—that explanation lies, at one level, in the kind of historical considerations we were discussing in the first chapter of this book and, at the deeper level, in the mysterious providence of God and therefore as far beyond the reach of our "explanations" as God's thoughts are beyond our thoughts and his ways beyond our ways. No, I am not trying to explain why Jesus died, but rather what the Cross came to stand for in the life of the Church. We are thinking, therefore, about the whole meaning and effect of the whole event of Christ. The case is not that the crucifixion of Jesus made the event significant, as all "theories" of the atoning death assume. Do I need to say again that it is *God* who made the event significant, and that it is impossible for us to explain—and perhaps presumptuous for us to try to explain—just how he did so or to identify the precise locus of his action? The Cross is significant, not as the source of the meaning of the event, but as the symbol of it. We are considering now, as we were in the preceding chapter also, some of the aspects of this significance—some of what is involved in our accepting the Cross as the symbol of the entire event. Thus to accept it, we are saying, means among other things seeing that suffering can be creative and redemptive.

The author of the Epistle to the Ephesians speaks of Jesus as having "slain the enmity" and "led captivity captive" (K.J.V.). Fastened to a cross, he is the giver of freedom; being killed by hatred, he gives love; dying, he offers life. This is but the truth about the death of Christ—the way it has actually worked; perhaps the way in which, beyond our understanding, it had to work out or be worked out. Maybe it is true that only the slain can finally slay enmity and only the captured can finally end captivity, that the love that suffers evil can alone conquer evil. It is not possible for us in this world fully or constantly to believe that; and if we think we do, we deceive ourselves. But the Cross will not let us forget that it may be true, and there will be times when we shall seem to see quite clearly that it is not only true, but one of the few glimpses we are given of the final truth, the truth that is beyond all our relative and partial truths, the very truth of God.

Accepting the Cross means also recognizing that we stand under an obligation which is beyond any possible measurement. We are commanded to *take up* our cross. This is not merely a verbal command of Jesus of Nazareth which happens to have been recorded in the Gospel. It is the word of the Cross itself. Taking up the cross means denying ourselves, not in the sense of denying things to ourselves, but in the sense of denying the self itself, of actually living around another center than our own interests—indeed of dying to self that we may live to God. How can we measure—much less, measure up to—such an obligation? Paul could say that he had been crucified with Christ, that he bore in his body the marks of the Lord Jesus, even that he made up in his own suffering what was lacking in the suffering of Christ. Committed to

170

the service of God in a way most of us hardly dream of and bearing trials and deprivations in that service such as most of us cannot even imagine, Paul had infinitely more right than we to say such things. But even so, do we not wonder at his saying them? However that may be, we know that we shall never be able to say such things ourselves. We find a certain comfort perhaps in Luke's variant reading, "Take up [your] cross daily," or "day by day." At first, this may seem to make the saying even harder, as of course it does. But looked at in a different way, it may seem to presuppose and to make some allowance for our weakness and our failures: We shall not be able to bear our cross with constancy; but we must not fail, when we let it fall, to take it up again. We must carry our cross till we fall; then rising we must grasp it again. For on such fidelity depends the whole meaning of our lives. Only by losing our life can we find it; only by "dying daily" can we know even now the meaning of life everlasting.

But accepting the Cross means relying finally upon the love of God, the love poured out in Christ and symbolized inevitably and forever by his bitter death. The obligation of which I have been speaking is so great only because it is an obligation laid on us by so great a love. One cannot know how much God asks of us except as one knows in that same moment how much he loves us. To know how much one lacks is to know how much God has already given. Really to hunger after righteousness is already to have been filled. To be able to feel the meaning of our sin as sin against God's love is already to have repented and already to have been forgiven. Needless to say, we cannot know the full dimensions of either our duty or God's love; but the one answers fully to the other, and in the measure we know the one we know the other.

This love of God is also the ground of a mighty hope. What

God has begun in us, he will surely finish. Having loved us, he will love us to the end—and on beyond any end our finitude permits us to imagine. "Christ being raised from the dead will never die again; death no longer has dominion over him" (Rom. 6:9); and to receive the love of God poured out in him is to share not only in his death but also in his resurrection. The Cross is not the *end* of all things, but their *center,* and therefore the symbol of a purpose of God which runs through all creation from the beginning to that "fullness of time" when he shall have "delivered us from the dominion of darkness and transferred us to the kingdom of his beloved Son, in whom we have redemption, the forgiveness of sins" (Col. 1:13).

From time to time Christians celebrate together the Church's deep remembrance of the death of Christ, expressing in symbolic action their participation in the body of his crucifixion and in the blood of his perfect sacrifice. God knows we are not worthy; we have let Christ die alone. But though we have failed to bear our cross, he did not fail to bear his. And for all our sin, past, present, and future, we do not profane the body of our Lord if only, each time we fall beneath our cross, we grasp the foot of his and take the love God offers us in him.

APPENDIX

APPENDIX

A Note on Rudolf Bultmann
and "Demythologization"

READERS of my two small books *On the Meaning of Christ* and *Criticism and Faith* [1] not infrequently ask me as to the extent to which I share the opinions of our great German contemporary Rudolf Bultmann. The question does me honor in suggesting that my views bear any resemblance, or stand in any significant relation, to his; but it also embarrasses me because it forces me to confess that at the time I wrote the two books, while familiar with some of Bultmann's critical writings, I had not read any of his hermeneutical or theological works. My friend and colleague Paul Tillich gave me several years ago a copy of *Kerygma und Mythos*,[2] in which Bultmann's famous essay on "demythologizing" was published. I read this essay with the greatest sympathy and with the realization that my own work might have been less inadequate if I had read it sooner. No reader of the present book, not to speak of the two earlier writings, would need to be told that this would be my

[1] Respectively: New York: Charles Scribner's Sons, 1947; and Nashville: Abingdon Press, 1952.

[2] H. W. Bartsch, ed. (Hamburg: Herbert Reich, 1948). The volume has since been translated into English by R. H. Fuller, *Kerygma and Myth* (London: S.P.C.K., 1953).

reaction. Bultmann speaks for many students of the New Testament in our generation, and in most significant respects he speaks for me.

What I feel in the way of misgiving or objection can be expressed perhaps in the form of three questions. The first is this: Does "demythologizing," as Bultmann proposes it, imply the dispensability of myth in the communicating of the Christian message; or does it mean only a recognition of its character as such? I am not as clear about Bultmann's position at this point as I should like to be. It is true that he says plainly enough: "As for mythology in the original sense, I maintain not only that we can dispense with it, but that it is essential to do so." But just what does he mean by this? He insists that the mythological cannot be eliminated from the New Testament but that it must be interpreted. Does he mean that the gospel can be interpreted so exhaustively in nonmythological terms that the myths are no longer needed in the preaching? Here is a crucial question. Is Bultmann only asking that the mythological be recognized both as being mythological and as standing for something empirically real? In that event, *so far as "demythologizing" itself, or as such, is concerned,* he is saying only what many scholars have been saying for a long time; and one must find any novelty in his position, not in the insistence upon demythologizing as such, but in his particular way of doing it—that is, in his way of defining either the empirical reality which the myths are seeking to express and convey (and Bultmann does have, of course, his own way of defining this reality, namely, in terms derived in considerable part from the existentialist philosophy) or else the relationship in which the reality and the myths stand to each other. But the repercussions of Bultmann's proposal, as well as the use of the term "demythologization" to designate it, would seem to indicate that he was understood to be urging nothing less than the dispensability of myth as a mode of the expression and communication of the Christian faith.

If Bultmann's "demythologizing" really means dispensing with myth, then I should dissent on two grounds: first, on the very general ground that if one is going to talk at all about what seems to the religious person to be disclosed in his experience, one must resort to mythological terms, or at any rate to highly symbolic terms, of one sort or another; and second, on the more specific, and for me more decisive, ground that the important Christian myths have been historically developed for the expression and communication of distinctively Christian concrete meanings, and that these meanings and these myths are inextricably involved with one another. For example, as we have seen, the forgiveness of God, as it is known in the Christian community, can be represented in its concreteness and particularity only by the story of God's sending his Son into the world to suffer for our sin. The myths both of Christ's sacrifice and of his victory answer to empirical realities within the historical community which for historical reasons, if for no other, can be designated and symbolized in no other way. Such myths belong to the very existence of the historical Church, and whatever validity and worth are ascribed to the Church itself can be ascribed to them.

This reference to the Church leads to the second question: Does not Bultmann slight its importance in his discussion of myth? The word occurs hardly at all in his essay in *Kerygma and Myth*. It may be objected that the reality of the Church is taken for granted, but still the fact that a discussion of Christian myth can be carried on with so little explicit reference to it is significant. The so-called Christ-event, it seems to me, tends to be for Bultmann an individual affair, rather than being a historical event in the true sense. To be sure, the event in its fullness, we will agree, did not occur publicly, "in the world," but it is just as true that it did not happen to individuals in their existential aloneness. It occurred in the midst of a group of persons and within a common or corporate life and, in so far as it may still be said to occur, it occurs there still. The "Christ-event" was in its issue, and therefore in its essence, the coming into existence of the Church; and this can be thought of as an objective historical event in the way the existential moment of faith cannot be. The myths came into being concurrently with the Church itself and were thus a part of the event itself. Radically to "demythologize"—that is, to destroy the Christian myths—would imply the destruction of the Church and therefore the denial of the event. To describe the salvation in Christ without the use of the historically developed myths would be impossible; one would be speaking of some other salvation or of no salvation at all. To *recognize* the myths as being myths is, of course, quite another thing.

Closely related to this question about the Church is our third question—a question about the adequacy of Bultmann's treatment of the Resurrection. For him the Resurrection is to be understood as "pure myth," as an attempt to convey the meaning of the Cross. "If the event of Easter Day," he writes, "is in any sense a historical event additional to the event of the cross, it is nothing else than the rise of faith in the risen Lord, since it is this faith which led to the apostolic preaching. The resurrection itself is not an event in past history." Now it would seem to me that when the creation of the Church is clearly recognized as being the true culmination, the essential meaning, of the entire Christ-event, a new dimension of ob-

jective truth is imparted to the resurrection of Christ, so that
we become able to speak of it as belonging to history rather
than to mythology only. If the resurrection of Jesus, the coming
of the Spirit, and the creation of the Church are recognized as
being three ways of referring to the same occurrence, there can
be no doubt as to the objective character of that occurrence—
that is, from the Church's own point of view. A new community
—that is, a new kind of shared life embodied in a new historically created society—did come into being. If in it the Spirit
is known, then the Spirit must be thought of as "coming."
If in it Christ is recognized as present, then he must be thought
of as "risen from the dead."

Although Bultmann is undoubtedly right in emphasizing
the inseparableness in the kerygma of the death of Jesus and
his resurrection—one "single, indivisible cosmic event"—I
think he does not do full justice to the Resurrection in its
own right. In effect he subordinates the Resurrection to the
Cross. What happened objectively was the Cross. The Resurrection is the realized meaning of that happening. "When he
suffered death, Jesus was already the Son of God and his death
by itself was a victory over the power of death." One wonders
whether Bultmann means just this—that is, whether he regards
this as an adequate account of the primitive faith at this point.
It is true, as we have seen, that one of the ways in which the
early Church sought to express the empirical meaning of the
event was the story of Jesus' victory over the evil powers; and
because the Cross was taken as a symbol of the whole event,
this victory was located there. But can we legitimately press the
myth so far as to make it mean that the actual dying of Jesus
was itself the victory over death? Does it not rather say that
he "loosed the [cords] of death," not simply by dying (although
he could not have loosed the cords if he had not first been

bound by them), but by rising from the dead? In a word, I believe that, unless we break rather decisively with the New Testament, the Resurrection has to be thought of as an occurrence distinct from the death, and that without this second occurrence (as indeed without other occurrences which also belonged to the event) the death could not have had the meaning it had. The Resurrection is not simply the meaning of the Cross, as Bultmann says; it is, along with the memory of the earthly life, the *source* of that meaning.

It is sometimes said that the "historicity of the Resurrection is established by the existence of the Christian Church." To me that argument, as it is usually presented, is entirely without validity; but taken in another way it is profoundly true. If the meaning of the sentence is that men formed the Church because they had first become convinced of Jesus' resurrection and that it is impossible to conceive of their doing so without this prior conviction, then the argument must, I think, be rejected. At best, all that would be demonstrated by it is the conviction of the disciples, not the fact of the Resurrection itself. But if the truth is, not that men formed the Church because they had come to believe in the Resurrection, but that they believed in the Resurrection because they actually found themselves members of the Church, then the existence of the Church does become evidence—the only evidence and the altogether adequate evidence—of the Resurrection. I would agree with Bultmann that the Easter event cannot be demonstrated in the same way the Crucifixion can be; but I would find the difference, not in the fact that the Crucifixion is an objective event in the ordinary sense whereas the Resurrection is not, but rather in the fact that the Crucifixion was, in the bare factual sense, a matter of public knowledge, while the

Resurrection was known only within the experience of the Church.

If by the "resurrection of Christ" one means an incident in the past, something that happened at a given time and place to the man Jesus, then it seems to me that we must recognize that it is only an inference from the essential life of the Church. The Church affirmed the Resurrection in this sense, not in the final resort because of "evidences," whether in the form of the empty tomb or of visionary experiences, but because of its own existence as a community of memory and the Spirit. The one remembered was not remembered only; he was alive and present. He must, therefore, have risen from the dead. But as will already have appeared, the resurrection of Christ means more than an incident in the past; it means the continuing realized identity of the one remembered with the one still known. For the Church to deny the Resurrection would be for it to deny its own existence, its own life as the community of the living Lord, who is also remembered. Now it is clear that when we talk in this way, we are talking as Christians and that the kind of argument implied would have no validity for anyone who did not share in the experience of the Christian Church. But it is my position that only such a one can know that the Resurrection took place or indeed can know what the Resurrection really means. This may be, in a general way, what Bultmann is saying, but I do not think it is exactly what he is saying. The difference lies, it seems to me, in the greater emphasis some of us would place upon the existence of the Church, and, it is important to add, upon the promise, both for history and for what lies beyond history, which that existence holds. For the Resurrection is the ground of our hope as well as the seal of our faith. The Church is "the colony of heaven"; the Spirit, which constitutes and informs it, is the "earnest of our inheritance" (K.J.V.).

Bultmann describes the "one event," which is the burden of the preaching, as "Jesus Christ, his cross and resurrection," the Resurrection being simply the Cross itself as its significance was (and is) existentially received by the believer. I should say that the event to which Christian faith looks back is both more complex and more objective than this. The coming into being of the Church was a quite objective fact, and that fact was not only the culmination of the event (and therefore what is essentially meant by the Resurrection), but it was the essential meaning of the event iself. The event as it developed in time *was* the Church gradually growing into existence. The culmination of the event *was* the culmination of this process of growth in the creation of the Church as a distinctive self-conscious community. The Resurrection *was* this new creation. To think of it so is to recognize its objective character, even though its concrete meaning can by definition be known only from within the new community itself.

But having said so much by way of questioning or criticizing Bultmann's views, or what I understand as Bultmann's views, I return to my original affirmation of admiration and sympathy. Bultmann has asked the right questions—questions which cannot be handled without some kind of radical dealing with the New Testament mythology.

Index of Scripture References

THE DEATH OF CHRIST

INDEX

Index of Names and Subjects

187

Death of Jesus. *See also* Crucifixion of
Jesus *and* Cross, the
Demytholigizing, 175 ff.
Divinity of Jesus, 70, 122-23
Docetism, 70
Dodd, C. H., 39-40, 44-45, 103-4, 153
Domitian, 138
Drama in New Testament, 19, 141-42,
151 ff.
Duncan, G. S., 60 ff., 63 ff., 93

Early Church
creativity of, 42-43, 45, 53, 109-10, 128
and the Gospels, 38-39, 41-42
and Judaism, 23 ff.
persecution of, 22, 137-38
preaching in, 19, 43
Ecstasy, 69, 114
Ehrhardt, Arnold, 26
Enoch 1-36, I, 55
Enoch 91-104, I, 55
Enoch, parables of, 57 ff., 92, 103-4
Esdras, II, 57 ff.
Eusebius, 116
Event of Christ, the, 50-51, 127 ff.,
131 ff., 157, 159-60, 177-78
Eyewitness testimony, value of, 47 ff.

Farmer, W. R., 27, 82, 117
Filson, F. V., 59
Foakes-Jackson, F. J., 104
Forgiveness of God, 150, 152, 155, 169
Fourth Gospel, character of, 42-43, 111,
130, 141-42
France, Anatole, 22
Fuller, R. H., 87, 103, 120, 175

Gentile mission, 23, 28
Gethsemane, 75, 112
Glasson, T. F., 58
Goodspeed, E. J., 80-81
Gospel and the Gospels, 127 ff.
Gospels, different conceptions of, 37 ff.
Grant, F. C., 87, 101, 139-40

Habakkuk, 55

Héring, J., 79, 96-97
Herod, trial before, 21, 24
High priest, Jesus before, 24-25
Historical career in Event, importance
of, 122, 132-33
Humanity of Jesus, 46, 56, 65, 69-70,
81, 111, 122-23, 132, 136-37, 141

Ignatius, 138
Inner life of Jesus, 110 ff.
Ius gladii, 25

Jeans, Sir James, 166
Jeremias, J., 25, 48, 102-3, 104
Jewish War, the, 22-23, 26 ff., 117
Joel, 55
John the Baptist, 120
Johnson, James Weldon, 46
Josephus, 21, 116-17
Judaism and early Church, 23 ff.

Kingdom of God, 18, 27 ff., 112, 117-18,
119
Klausner, Joseph, 97
Kraeling, Carl, 62
Kuhn, K. G., 55-56

Lagrange, M. J., 116
Lake, Kirsopp, 104
Last Supper, 48, 120
Law, New Testament conception of,
153
Lietzmann, H., 25, 87, 97

Maccabees, 27, 117
Maccabees, I, 55
Maccabees, IV, 73-74
Manson, T. W., 59 ff., 63 ff., 69, 93, 116
Manson, William, 40
Mark, theology of, 47, 100-101, 161-62
Martyrs, 113 ff., 161-62
McArthur, H. K., 59
Messiah
different conceptions of, 54 ff., 117
evidences of Jesus' self-identification
with, 57, 77 ff.

INDEX OF NAMES AND SUBJECTS